# THE ROOF OF THE WORLD

## Mohamed Amin · Duncan Willetts · Brian Tetley

Camerapix Publishers International
NAIROBI

Acknowledgements
The aerial photography in this book would not have been possible without the support
of the Pakistan Army Aviation Command. In particular, we are indebted to Majors
Amir Sanjar, Mohamed Farooq, and Javed Ahmed for flying helicopters through the
high passes around some of the world's mightiest mountains. It requires very special
skills. So does climbing them and for this we owe special thanks to Major Sher Khan.
He has climbed several major peaks including Gasherbrum II in 1982 with Reinhold
Messner, and Nanga Parbat. His mountaineering skills and advice are a major
contribution.

First published 1989 by
Camerapix Publishers International,
P.O. Box 45048,
Nairobi, Kenya

© Camerapix 1989

ISBN 0 869 828 05 4

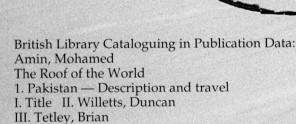

British Library Cataloguing in Publication Data:
Amin, Mohamed
The Roof of the World
1. Pakistan — Description and travel
I. Title   II. Willetts, Duncan
III. Tetley, Brian

This book was designed and produced by
Camerapix Publishers International,
P.O. Box 45048,
Nairobi, Kenya

Design: Craig Dodd

Typesetting : Halpen Graphic Communication Limited

Half-title: K2, the world's second-highest mountain. Title: Three majestic faces of The Roof of The World, from left
— Trango, Baltoro Cathedral, Lobsang, and Broad Peak. Contents page: The 2,000-year-old 'Silk Road' footpath
winds over one of the highest plateaux in the world — the frozen Deosai Plains, at 14,000 feet. Pages 6-7: Shigar
Village at the western foot of the Masherbrum range. Pages 8-9: Riakot face of 26,660-feet-high Nanga Parbat. Pages
10-11: Trekkers in Concordia beneath 20,466-feet-high Marble Peak, with K-2 in background. Pages 12-13: 25,660-
feet-high Masherbrum rises above the Yermanendu Glacier.
Endpapers: Satellite picture of the Roof of the World

# Contents

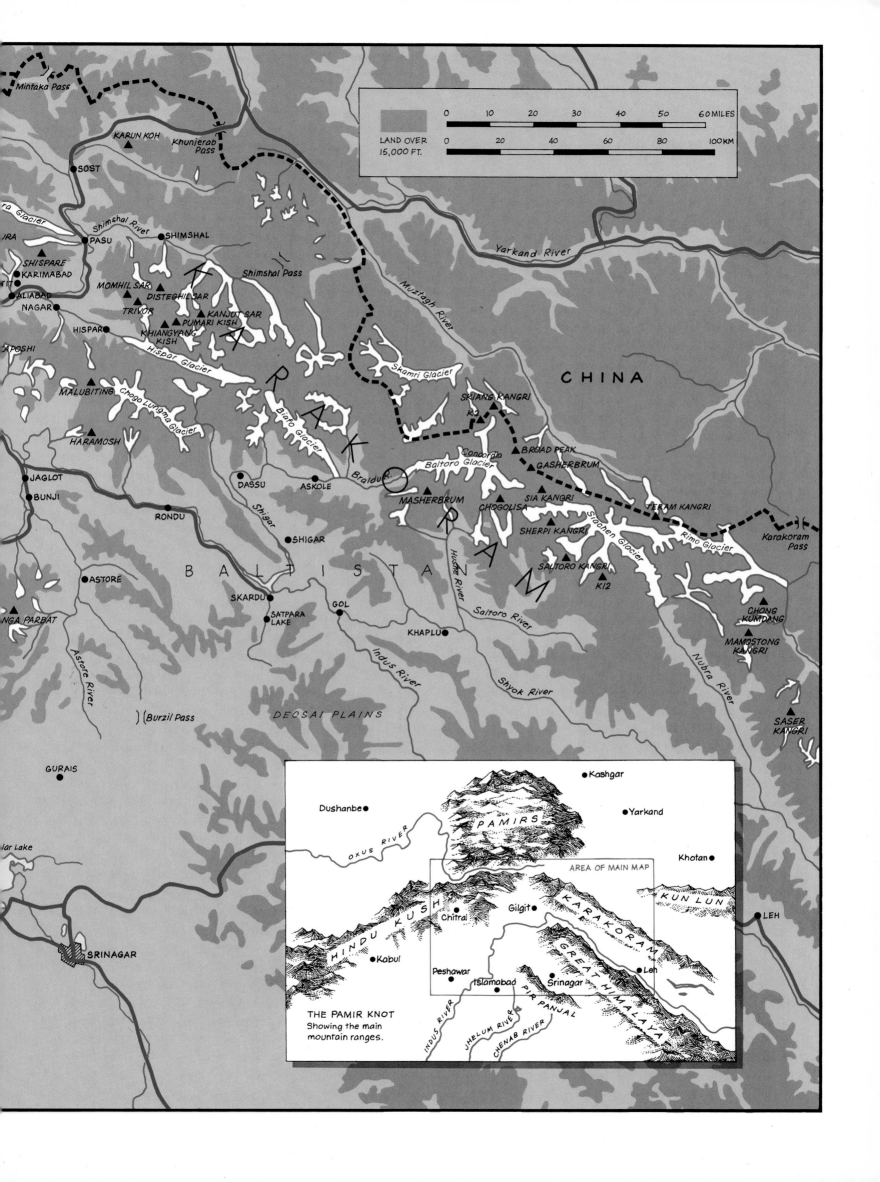

Mintaka Pass

KARUN KOH ▲
Khunjerab Pass
SOST ●

ra Glacier
Shimshal River
PASU ●    SHIMSHAL ●
IRA
▲
SHISPARE ▲
KIT ●    KARIMABAD
ALIABAD ●
NAGAR ●
MOMHIL SAR ▲
DISTEGHIL SAR ▲
TRIVOR ▲    KANJUT SAR ▲
HISPAR ●    PUMARI KISH ▲
KHIANGYANG KISH ▲
APOSHI
Hispar Glacier

Shimshal Pass

Yarkand River

Muztagh River

Skamri Glacier

CHINA

K A R A K

MALUBITING ▲
Choga Lungma Glacier
HARAMOSH ▲

Biafo Glacier

SKIANG KANGRI ▲
K2 ▲

JAGLOT ●
BUNJI ●
RONDU ●
DASSU ●    ASKOLE ●    Braldu ○
Shigar
SHIGAR ●

Concordia
Baltoro Glacier
BROAD PEAK ▲
GASHERBRUM ▲

O R A M

MASHERBRUM ▲
CHOGOLISA ▲    SIA KANGRI ▲
SHERPI KANGRI ▲    Siachen Glacier
SALTORO KANGRI ▲
K12 ▲

TERAM KANGRI ▲
Rimo Glacier
Karakoram Pass

B A L T I S T A N
Husthe River

ASTORE ●
SKARDU ●
SATPARA LAKE    GOL ●
KHAPLU ●
Saltoro River

NGA PARBAT
Indus River
Shyok River

Nubra River

CHONG KUMDANG ▲

MAMOSTONG KANGRI ▲

Astore River
(Burzil Pass)
DEOSAI PLAINS

GURAIS ●

SASER KANGRI ▲

lar Lake

SRINAGAR ●

THE PAMIR KNOT
Showing the main mountain ranges.

Dushanbe ●    ● Kashgar
OXUS RIVER    PAMIRS    ● Yarkand
● Khotan
AREA OF MAIN MAP
KUN LUN
HINDU KUSH    ● Chitral    ● Gilgit    KARAKORAM
● Kabul    GREAT HIMALAYA
● Peshawar    ● Leh
● Islamabad    ● Srinagar    ● Leh
INDUS RIVER    JHELUM RIVER    CHENAB RIVER    PIR PANJAL

# 1 Introduction: Where

# Continents Collide

From a satellite picture taken thousands of kilometres out in space, ridged and crumpled, their green surfaces dappled dark brown, the mountain ranges of the Asian subcontinent look like the leaves of a fern. Distance lends serenity to the ruggedness of the place Arab geographers named 'Bam-i-Dunya', at the heart of which is the Pamir Knot, the world's umbilical cord. Tenaciously, its drawstring pulls together great and majestic crests without their like anywhere.

Here, amid wind- and snow-ravaged gorge and peak, two ancient continents collide, and their mighty offspring — the Himalaya, Karakoram, Hindu Kush, and Pamir mountain ranges — jostle, thrust, and heave in titanic and unrelenting struggle.

After sixty-five million years of encounter, the continental plate of India is still seeking supremacy, gaining ground at the rate of around five centimetres a year as it grinds into the Asian continental plate, edging the mountains another millimetre or two higher year by year.

Where the tides of the Tethys Sea once ebbed and flowed, now K-2 — of all the world's mountains second only to Everest — shreds the jet stream at 28,269 feet. At its foot stretches another wonder of the world, Concordia: a rippling, pitted, pockmarked river of ice, where great glaciers slide and slither together before separating to go their different ways. Like a proscenium, Concordia is part of the main stage of a natural amphitheatre that has no equal.

This is The Roof of the World. On every side, within a distance of twenty-four kilometres, rise up ten of the world's thirty highest peaks. As graphic in name as they are foreboding in majesty, the Himalaya translate as 'The Abode of the Snows'; the Karakoram, the 'Black Gravel Mountains'; and the Hindu Kush, 'The Slayer of Indians'.

Two more ranges, by unique comparison minor in size, thrust their sinews and limbs into the Pamir Knot: the Pir Panjal with its peaks of just over 20,000 feet, and China's Celestial Mountains, the Kun Lun. Where these six ranges merge in a 1,000-kilometre-long by 500-kilometre-wide swathe, they form what many regard as the most impressive landscape in the world.

Much of this dramatic locale falls within the borders of northern Pakistan, which holds five of the world's fourteen highest mountains — those over 8,000 metres (26,250 feet) — and more than sixty higher than 7,000 metres (23,000 feet). It was here sixty-five million years ago that the ancient continents of India and Asia first came into geological conflict and then fused in uneasy consummation; their shuddering energies centred on the ever-moving citadels of the six mountain chains.

Bounded in the west by Afghanistan, separated from the Soviet Union in the north-west by a narrow neck of land nowhere wider than fifty kilometres, China to the north and Indian-held Kashmir in the east, northern Pakistan, tumultuous and magnificent, takes the breath of all who fall under its spell.

Opposite: Villagers in Shimshal Valley live spartan existence during long winter's night awaiting burgeoning spring and the brief respite of warming summer sun.

Previous pages: Pitted and pockmarked river of ice — Biafo Glacier streams eastward for more than fifty-nine kilometres from the Roof of The World. Linked at its source with the westward flowing Hispar Glacier, from tail to tail their combined length totals 122 kilometres.

Overleaf: Majestic Pamir mountains ring the lost horizons valley of Shimshal above the Mulumgutti Glacier.

Previous pages: Snowclad peaks in the background, the mighty Indus River has gouged a deep and dramatic gorge through the Roof of the World.

Left: Youngsters revel in the brief but warm summer sun that turns Gulmit Valley into a blaze of blossoms.

Left: Young boy in the remote village of Misghar near the Chinese border.

Opposite: Howling, banshee winds and their razor's edge combine with ice and time to shape these fascinating rock sculptures along the upper Hunza Valley just before Sost.

Even today, much of the region has yet to be fully explored and mapped. From the earliest accounts down to the present day, the Pamir Knot and the ranges it ties together — remote, isolated, and largely uninhabited — remain an enigma.

One of the first to climb along the eaves, cornices, and slopes of The Roof of the World was the great Chinese traveller and Buddhist pilgrim, Huan Tsang, remarking that 'The Lake of the Great Dragon', Sar-i-Kol, was the most splendid place on earth.

The thirteenth-century Venetian trader and traveller, Marco Polo, who left his name behind on the magnificent-horned wild sheep of these reaches, may well have trod the same path and marvelled, too, at the glory of this lake. It was rediscovered six centuries later by Lieutenant John Wood, an Indian Navy officer searching for the source of the Oxus, 'that great parent stream of humanity'.

Another Chinese traveller, Fah Hian, recorded his awe. 'Steep crags and precipices constantly intercept the way. These mountains are like walls of rock, standing up 10,000 feet in height. On looking over the edge, the sight becomes confused, and then on advancing the foot loses its hold, and you are lost.'

And his compatriot, Sung Yun, sighed, 'For a thousand *li* there are overhanging crags, 10,000 fathoms high, towering up to the very heavens.'

Determined to discover the true source of the Oxus, whose 'waters tell of forgotten peoples and whisper secrets of unknown lands . . . believed to have rocked the cradle of our race', Lord Curzon, a future British Viceroy in India, followed in Wood's footsteps in 1894. 'As regards the scenery,' he commented , 'its main characteristic is the almost total absence of horizontal lines.'

John Biddulph, a British Indian Army officer who, during four years on special duty in Gilgit between 1877 and 1881, travelled through most of the region, noted that it had attracted little attention. 'The apparent neglect has been caused by the almost inaccessible nature of the country. In no other part of the world, probably, is there to be found such a large number of lofty mountains within so confined a space. This mass of mountain is intersected by numerous deep valleys, and these, owing to some peculiar geological formation which I have not remarked in other parts of the Himalayas, are generally narrower at their mouths, than higher up. It is not unusual to see among them valleys of from 100 to 300 miles in length . . . with an embouchure so narrow that it is difficult to find a pathway beside the torrent which issues between overhanging rocks.'

The man who surveyed K-2, Lieutenant Henry Haversham Godwin-Austen, drew sketches which, John Keay remarks in *When Men and Mountains Meet*, 'illustrates superbly the incredible perpendicularity of the central Karakorams. In the valleys the eye never pans. Always it is climbing. The

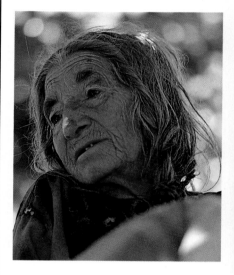

Above: Mineral-rich waters and an almost perpetual diet of dried fruit combined with high altitude have given the people of the Hunza Valley an enviable and proven reputation for longevity.

neck aches from the unaccustomed action, and the sky is just a slit directly overhead'.

And again . . . 'no one has ever succeeded in conveying to those who have not known the Himalayas any conception of their size. To talk of mountains nearly ten times the size of Snowdon [a British mountain] or twice the height of Mont Blanc means nothing. Homely comparisons only belittle the grandeur . . . no attempt at a scale can convey the effect of such mighty scenery. . . .

'A vast array of snow-clad peaks would rise from the blanket of mist in the valleys. An impossible, unearthly world of the purest beauty etched out of a deep blue sky, it seemed quite untouched by man.'

These are among the many who found, and continue to find, the mountains and their hidden valleys and passes almost impenetrable and inhospitable, although Marco Polo was struck by the rich highland pastures which, he reported, could fatten a starving cow within ten days. But the cold and rarefied air, he discovered, meant his camp-fires burned less brightly, causing his food to be undercooked.

The Hindu Kush, rising out of parched and arid Afghanistan, forms the westernmost buttress of this formidable citadel, its rumpled sterile flanks, almost without cover, climbing ever higher into the sky as they advance towards the main bastion. Dominated by the glaciers of the world's forty-first-highest mountain, 25,290-foot-high Tirich Mir, the treeless slopes are bounded in the north by that river of mystery, the Oxus, which rushes north to flow into Russia's Aral Sea, a salt lake next in size to Victoria in Africa. Beyond the Oxus, lie the rocky domes of the Pamirs.

Meeting the Pamirs from the east is the Kun Lun range, dominated by the heights of Ulugh Mustagh, 25,355 feet, and Bokalik Tagh, 25,328 feet. Within the junction formed by these three systems lies the fourth range, the Karakoram — creating the actual knot that forms the Concordia amphitheatre dominated by K-2 and 26,470-foot-high Gasherbrum I; Broad Peak, 26,400 feet; Gasherbrum II, 26,360 feet; Gasherbrum III, 26,041 feet; and Gasherbrum IV, 26,000 feet. In close attendance are Disteghil Sar, 25,868 feet; Khiangyang Kish, 25,760 feet; Masherbrum, 25,660 feet; Rakaposhi, 25,550 feet; Batura Mustagh, 25,540 feet; Kanjut Star, 25,460 feet; Saltoro Kangri, 25,400 feet; the unclimbed Peak Thirty-five, 25,279 feet; Batura Mustagh II, 25,361 feet; and 25,329-foot high Trivor.

The Karakoram boast more 25,000-foot-high mountains, too, including Saser Kangri, 25,170 feet; Chogolisa SW, 25,148 feet; N.E. Gipfel, 25,110 feet; and Shispare or Batura, 25,000 feet — and many more above at least 24,000 feet.

Here the mighty Himalaya, seemingly overshadowed, fade away. But the range holds one final, stupendous surprise to spring on the unsuspecting — Nanga Parbat, westernmost anchor of the greatest mountain range in the

Opposite: Verdant terraced fields of Minapin Village, perched on a tiny plateau in the shadows of Rakaposhi in the Hunza Valley.

Previous pages: The source of the Baltoro Glacier beneath 24,351-feet-high Sia Kangri. The ridge to the right of the peak is the 19,600-feet-high Conway Saddle which leads over to the head of the seventy-five-kilometre-long Siachen Glacier. At extreme right is the north-western shoulder of 23,990-feet-high Golden Throne.

Overleaf: Craggy peaks surround remote Misghar, centuries ago the major southern gateway for the Silk Route before the long climb over the Khunjerab Pass.

world, huge, vast, and deadly, climbing 26,660 feet into the clinging lenticular clouds which characterize 'The Naked Mountain'. These misty phantoms, on a mountain massif which makes its own weather and is often mistaken as an entire range, were described by the late Sherpa Tenzing Norgay, conqueror of Everest with Sir Edmund Hillary, as 'a cloud of fear . . . of death'. Only 190 kilometres separates the crest of Nanga Parbat from that of K-2.

As a final thread in the umbilical cord, the Pir Panjal coils northward from the south-east to knot itself into the Himalaya; though serving, at least in height alone, as little more than foothills, the range provides some of the most fertile and hauntingly beautiful alpine panoramas anywhere in the world. The northern extremity of the flanks of the Pir Panjal provide the final, almost delicate, touch to this incredible landscape.

In this perpendicular wilderness, treacherous and forbidding, life is hard. Not surprisingly, fewer than one per cent of the world's ninth most populous nation live in the 140,000 square kilometres of northern Pakistan: but the proud and intricate cultures of those who do create a mosaic that is a colourful and priceless heritage.

Alone in their mountain fastnesses, cut off for centuries from any real contact with the outside world, these communities have maintained and enriched their traditions, uncorrupted by outside "civilizing" influences. Thus aided by nature in preserving their independence, even isolated from one another during long winter's night, they formed separate communities and for millenniums lived their separate lives within the same narrow limits. They existed much as their forbears did, unaffected by the changes taking place around them and only slightly distracted by internal strife and feuding.

Only in the closing stages of the twentieth century, with swift new lines of communication, have the people of these lonely former kingdoms of the mountains and the valleys begun to move into the mainstream of national life — and at a pace suited to their hardy, independent life styles.

Yet in deep gorges beneath the glaciers, rivers wild and wonderful nourish tiny hamlets and villages like Hunza, the fabled *Shangri-la* from the pages of James Hilton's *Lost Horizon.* In these lost and hidden valleys hardy people till their precious soil and live far longer than the rest of us. This glittering mosaic of human cultures contains many different ethnic groups and tribes: some the descendants of Genghis Khan and Tamurlane, a main stock of Mongol, Aryan, and Turanian that here coalesces, homogenized by their common Islamic faith. There is one exception — the pagan Kalash who live in the lost valleys of Chitral.

The verdant, gentler hills of the Pir Panjal, including the incomparable Kaghan Valley; the moulded contours of the lower valleys of the Hindu Kush, like Swat and Chitral; mingling with the glories of the Himalaya, such as the Astore and Skardu valleys; ring out a perfect counterpoint to the harsh, forbidding grandeur of the Karakoram and Pamirs. Watered by the snowmelt

Above: Enduring tribute to the hundreds that died in the making of the Karakoram Highway

Overleaf: The riven, rippling surface of the Baltoro Glacier, one of the world's great rivers of ice that streams down from Concordia for almost sixty kilometres.

and monsoon runoffs, great rivers like the Jehlum and the Indus are born in these mountains and gather momentum to bestow their bounty downstream on a land brought to fecundity by the spring and summer sun.

Though vast reserves of water are locked within the frozen embrace of mountain peak and glacier, much of the region — particularly the Hindu Kush and Karakoram — is barren desert: rugged rock and glacial debris, broken by sudden lush oases terraced out of the mountainside or tended on the valley floor. Elsewhere, in the north, however, the soil is productive and the seasons of spring and summer, though brief, an occasion for rejoicing as fruits, vegetables, grains, and flowers burst into colour and yield their harvest riches.

Throughout northern Pakistan, each day's travel brings constant revelation and the magic of incomparable vistas, breathtaking discoveries of snowy mountain crests, dynamic and colourful cultures, rare wildlife — like the ibex and the snow leopard — jade lakes and chuckling streams, dancing waterfalls, and pine-cloaked hills ablaze in summer with glorious alpine flowers.

Here is magnificence and memory to enchant all who witness it: the distant cascading roar of the Indus in flood heard against the melody of a wistful, whispering breeze eddying through a flower-filled highland meadow; the groaning, creaking agony of a glacier in motion heralding the first sight of that purest of mountains, the thrusting pyramid of K-2 as it breaks through its girdle of clouds to float disembodied, a marvellous phantom in the incredible blue of an early morning sky.

Some 150 million years ago it lay on the bed of a vast inland sea, the Tethys, and dinosaurs roamed its shores. As the earth cooled, newly-formed rock, forged out of its molten core, pushed upwards to form the Tibetan plateau. Slowly the inland sea drained away into a new river — the Indus, flowing north-west and then south. About fifty million years ago, the northern mass of Asia began to slip southward as the island continent of India moved northward.

Ten million years later they met, and the earth's crust, caught between these two irresistible forces, cracked, buckled, folded over, and arched itself up towards the sky. The greatest mountains on earth were born.

The northerly lowlands of Pakistan were demarcated by the baseline of foothills that stretch south-east from Peshawar to the Indian border. The western buttress of The Roof of the World, the Hindu Kush, diverted potential invaders and conquerors southward down to the Khyber Pass through which they marched on Peshawar and the Punjab plains.

Thus they were denied knowledge of the incomparable delights of those valleys, well-hidden, where it is best to begin any exploration of the delights that rest beneath The Roof of the World.

# 2 Over Hill and Dale

Arched close by Islamabad, running along the northern horizon, the pine-covered Margalla Hills form a stunning backdrop to Pakistan's federal capital which was built in the 1960s. These are the south-western foothills of the lovely Pir Panjal mountains, the chain that guards the southern flank of the western Himalaya. The pine trees that stand along the topmost ridges give these hills the look of a curved and fluttering eyelash, coy yet seductive, beckoning the traveller forward. From their crest you climb all the way to The Roof of the World.

The Margalla mark the southernmost boundary of a region of northern Pakistan which surely claims more beautiful and dramatic landscapes — natural and manmade — within its 10,000 square kilometres than any comparable area. Known as Hazara, the Pir Panjal also mark its eastern boundary and divide it from Azad Kashmir. The buttress of the Hindu Kush is its western flank and the Himalaya, where they lace into the Pamir Knot, form its northern boundary.

Hazara's creation began about 150 million years ago when, century after century, the Tethys sea began to narrow. Sixty-five million years ago sediments on the sea bed began to ruck and crumple and, compacting into mudstone, limestone, and sandstone, thrust upward into mountains and hills like the Margalla range.

Slowly, the ancient Tethys Sea began to drain away to the north-west, forming a new river only to find its way barricaded by the rising ramparts of the Pamir Knot. These changes were no sudden cataclysm but spread over hundreds of thousands of years. Around thirty million years ago, where the soft sea bed gave no foundation, Asia began to slip south, meeting the unyielding block of India.

Now, as the land rose, the river, one of the few natural features that survived this dramatic remodelling of the earth's surface, flowed swift and strong. But, diverted by the rising mass on its northern banks, it began to cut its way west and then southward through the mountains, forming what are now among the deepest gorges on earth — some more than 15,000 feet deep.

It was to become a river of human history and, as the Indus, gave its name to the new subcontinent. Running north-west out of the Tibetan plateau, in parallel with the Himalaya, it curved around the western flank of this great range, where the Pamir Knot was tied, to plunge into the deep rift between the Hindu Kush and the Pir Panjal and then southward over the great depression which begins at Hazara.

At least 6,000 feet deep and, some think, perhaps as much as 15,000 feet deep, it was a monumental basin in the earth's surface — a deep sea-filled gulf. But after the Indus ground, cut, and chiselled its way through these mountains, it flowed across Hazara and in the season of the floods began to deposit its silt — not only on the sea bed but on the shores on either side.

Lower downstream, where it is joined by its four tributaries, all flowing

Left: Holidaymakers revel in snow at Ayubia town.

Left: Bazaar in the main square of the hill town of Murree.

from the same mountain massifs, including the Jhelum that forms the eastern boundary of Hazara and Azad Kashmir, it eventually filled in the vast gulf to form the Punjab and the mass of what is now Pakistan. Such power to transform and reshape great natural features is beyond human comprehension.

But as you journey northward from Islamabad over the Margalla Hills to The Roof of the World you slowly begin to perceive, if not completely understand, the scale and dimensions of the world's most tumultuous landscapes.

For much of its journey through Hazara, the Indus and its valley form the district's western boundary, dividing it from Swat. At Tarbela, sixty-five kilometres north-west of Islamabad, where the Indus emerges from its last gorge, man has endeavoured to transform nature on a scale to match the awesome and restless energy of the planet's forces.

Between 1968 and 1971, at the base of the Gandghar Hills, construction crews built a massive 2.7-kilometre-wide, 469-foot-high, earth-filled rampart across the Indus to tame its raging waters and provide energy for national growth. Three times the size of the Aswan Dam in Egypt which harnessed the waters of the Nile, it was for many years the world's largest earth-filled dam. On either side engineers built two giant spillways — 116 metres wide and, again, the world's largest — to channel the late summer monsoon and snow melt onrush of the Indus flood waters past the barrier. They burst free of the lake down the spillways in a thundering torrent before crashing into deep plunge pools.

Backing up behind the dam, the Indus created one of the subcontinent's great lakes: several hundred square kilometres of water, 450 feet deep, ringed by hills. Villages and farms were inundated by the rising waters and where once cattle grazed and cereals were sown and reaped, now the harvest is fish. From its muddy shores, thousands ply the lake waters. This glistening lake with its green and pleasant landscape gives grace to mankind's conceit.

Looking as if it has lain there since the Indus first sprang free of its mountain prison, it stretches northwards along the feet of Hazara's Black Mountains for almost 100 kilometres.

Long before the World Bank-funded dam was built, the people of Tarbela knew well the power of the Indus. A century and a half ago, at Sazin on the northern border of Hazara with the Gilgit Agency, Nanga Parbat stirred in its long slumber and sent its lower slopes crashing down the mountainside, trapping the Indus floods behind a massive rampart of mountain rubble. A lake almost as large as the one now at Tarbela — extending more than eighty kilometres to the town of Gilgit — was formed behind this barrier. But a year later, in June 1841, when Nanga Parbat shuddered again in its sleep, the dam was breached.

Gathering momentum and height, a gigantic tidal wave bore down through

45

the narrow gorges for more than 160 kilometres until it spread out at Tarbela to race across the plains in a force so powerful it engulfed four towns and twenty villages, drowning many thousands and flooding the land around for thousands of square kilometres. An army record of the event at Tarbela reports:

*At two in the afternoon, the waters were seen by the soldiers encamped on the banks of the Indus to be coming down upon them, down the various channels, and to be swelling out of these to overspread the plain in a dark, muddy mass which swept everything before it. The camp was completely overwhelmed; 500 soldiers at once perished . . . trees and house were were swept away; every trace of civilization was swept away.*

The word Hazar, from which this region takes its name, is Farsi for a thousand, bestowed, it is said, by the thousand soldiers left behind by the great Mongolian warlord, Genghis Khan, or his successor Tamurlane, to colonize it after their conquests. Later the Mughal Emperors, who built a great empire from Aghanistan right across India, coveted it as a strategic fortress.

Encircled by mountains in all but the south where the River Jhelum flows down to the Punjab Plains, this fair and lovely greensward vale was also the easiest all-weather route from Peshawar to that Eden of their delight, the Vale of Kashmir. Below Tarbela, the road led across the Peshawar plains and along the banks of the River Dor to Abbottabad and then Manshera, where it forked eastward to Muzaffarabad, the westernmost flank of the Pir Panjal, to follow the Jhelum Valley to Kashmir.

With the decline of the Mughal Empire at the end of the seventeenth century, Hazara came under the ambiguous rule of the Pukhtun Durranis from Afghanistan finally passing to Ranjit Singh, the Sikh who ruled much of Punjab and north-west India through the eighteenth century and the early part of the nineteenth century. He wanted to secure the road to Kashmir, too, but like the British who followed, found the tribesmen of hill and plain unruly. In 1835, according to a contemporary report, a state of anarchy existed on the plains around Manshera where outlaws and highwaymen robbed and murdered innocent travellers; and villagers ringed their compounds with stockades of stout thorn hedges.

When the British took control in the mid-nineteenth century little had changed, nor did it do so for many years. Indeed, Kohistan district in northernmost Hazara remains one of the least changed places in all the world. It was for long a refuge for vagabonds, murderers, and criminals.

People of many different cultural complexions live in Hazara — some the descendants of the Swat Pukhtuns who sought refuge across the Black Mountains when they fled the Yusufzai clan which rampaged through Swat in the sixteenth century; the nomadic Gujars, the original pastoralists of this

Right: Graceful monument to the men who laid down their lives to build the Karakoram Highway at Thakot where it officially begins its long climb to the Khunjerab Pass.

Right: Stone monument indicates the vast distances that the Karakoram Highway climbs through the gorges that dissect the highest mountains on earth.

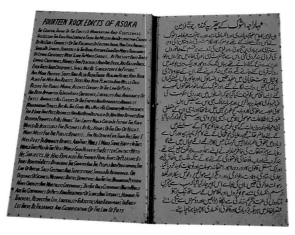

northern region, still tend their flocks and herds in the pastoral beauty of valleys like Kaghan, their women unveiled. And there are also the Dhunds, Saiads, and Ghakkars. The Pukhtuns live in the Gandghar Hills. In Kohistan the stock is a hybrid mixture of Pukhtun, Mongol, Chinese, Kamian, and Turkish.

From Islamabad, an aircraft carries you in minutes over the pine-crested brow of the Margalla Hills, rising in a series of parallel ridges, one after the other — each higher than the other, each ascending ever nearer to the mighty giants of Pakistan's northernmost territory — into Hazara and another world.

Beneath the plane lie the hidden charms of fertile valleys terraced with fields and mottled with villages on the banks of dancing streams and sparkling lakes. Glistening in the early morning sunlight is the great sweep of Tarbela Lake. Close by, nestling among lush, richly coloured fruit orchards and fields watered by the Dor River, is Haripur, a town whose name commemorates Ranjit Singh's most trusted general, Hari Singh. Ranjit despatched the general to Haripur in the early 1820s to quell Hazara and 'inflict severe chastisement' on its lawless tribes.

But in the Gandghar Hills Hari Singh came up against the Pukhtun Mishwanis, losing 500 men. He endured an uneasy tenure until 1834 when he was posted to Peshawar. Later, after the Sikh War of 1846, an Englishman, James Abbott, then thirty-nine, one of Sir Henry Lawrence's 'young men', was despatched as an 'adviser' to the Sikhs, but this role did not last long. In 1848 during the second Sikh War, he found himself cut off in Hazara while Chattar Singh, another Sikh General, held the lower end of the region around Hasan Abdal.

He took refuge with the Mishwanis and, described by Sir Henry as 'of the stuff of the true knight errant . . . ready at all times to sacrifice himself for his country or his friend', took an instant liking to their Pukhtun demeanour, courage, and sense of honour.

Attending a Mishwani council of elders, *jirga,* he asked them to stand by his side and fight the Sikhs with him. 'We swore we would,' an old survivor remembered to Sir Olaf Caroe in 1927, 'and there were tears in our eyes and a tear in Abbott Sahib's eyes, too.' Abbott then led them to the Margalla Pass to block the retreat of the Sikh invaders.

The Sikhs' English adversary became Hazara's first British proconsul and is best remembered in local folklore leading prayers in the town mosque, dressed in the long robes of Islam and with a long white beard. Leading two expeditions into the Black Mountains and the Kaghan Valley to put down insurgencies, he served as proconsul in Hazara until 1853 when he was posted to Calcutta in Bengal. It was Herbert Edwardes, his successor, who founded the town that bears Abbott's name, and Haripur became of secondary importance.

Midway between the two towns stands Havelian, where work began on the magnificent Karakoram Highway that traces the course of the old Silk Route into China, although as long ago as the last century its British-built predecessor stretched as far as Manshera. Virtually from sea level, this great highway climbs upwards for 1,287 kilometres to more than 16,000 feet at the Khunjerab Pass.

At Abbottabad, where it runs through the town like an arrow for many kilometres, it touches only 4,000 feet above sea level, a height which made the town a popular hot season hill retreat for India's British rulers. The 1980s has seen it develop both as a military town and tourist centre. Almost everywhere you go in this town, set at the southern end of the great bowl of the Rash plains, you meet the descendants of the Mughal armies — their twentieth-century training reflecting the proud martial heritage of their ancestors.

Ayub Khan had his summer retreat in Abbottabad, too. Frontier House, his old residence on a ridge overlooking the Rash plains, has an incongruous Chinese pagoda in the garden.

Abbottabad's old European suburb echoes the grand days of Empire. Climb up the hill through the bustling bazaar to the crest, where stands the old Anglican church and cemetery surrounded by pine-shaded villas, bungalows, and the mandatory colonial club. Though in need of repair, the church is still in occasional use. Borrow the key from the vicarage and walk inside. The stuff of Kipling springs to life. Plaques recording the lives and deaths of British officers and men far from home recall the days of death and glory on the North-West Frontier when, as Kipling wrote, there was:

> *A scrimmage in a Border Station —*
> *A canter down some dark defile —*
> *Two thousand pounds of education*
> *Drops to a ten rupee jazail —*
> *The Crammer's boast, the Squadron's pride.*
> *Shot like a rabbit in a ride.*

But for most death came through sickness and fever. The graveyard, peaceful and well kept, is a shrine to those who came to serve Queen and Empire never to return. There are also tiny graves — those of the children who never saw the shores of their homeland.

Today, enmity and recrimination forgotten in the pride of nationhood, the successors of the old Empire are welcomed with typical warmth and generosity and, with the tourist officers at the Pakistan Tourist Development Corporation office next to the church, plan their journey through Hazara and beyond — to idyllic places like Kaghan Valley and Kohistan.

Closer at hand, too, there are many places in which to enjoy the wonders of this unsurpassed landscape — in particular, the summer journey through Nathiagalli, untouched for centuries, to the hills and dales of Murree. Among the many glories of this region, on a forest plateau near Abbottabad is

Thandiani, set almost 9,000 feet above sea level.

It was once a thriving, cool retreat from the unbearable heat of the plains below. But then the old hill-station bungalows fell into ruin and the church was boarded up. Now, more than forty years after Pakistan's Independence, Thandiani is coming back into its own — it's isolation ended with the new road that cuts through ravines of fractured rock, terraced fields, and forest as it snakes its way to the top of the ridge.

For many who will never venture farther north this is truly The Roof of the World. The panorama draws the breath — in the dreamy haze of a summer's midday your gaze takes in the ribbon of the Jhelum River and the snowy crests of the Pir Panjal to the east, and to the north the grand vistas of the the mountains of Kohistan and the Kaghan Valley. Framing the foreground for the majestic pinnacle of far-distant Nanga Parbat, Kaghan Valley's highest peak, Malika Parbat, stands out against the azure sky in a bold relief of rock and snow.

And to the west, floating like a mirage on the summer sky, rise the Black Mountains; behind them the shadowy outline of the Hindu Kush. Southwest, across the shimmering plains beyond Abbottabad, glistens the ribbon of the Indus. And to the south, the forested slopes of the Gallis tempt the walker.

Any of the walks through the cool forest cathedral of dappled glade and fern, shadowy grove and trail, leads to promise fulfilled. Climb the trail to Hule ka Danna at the edge of the plateau, undefiled by man and his industry, and enjoy an even more glorious view of Nanga Parbat.

To savour the memorable delights of these hills many trek, for two days or more, from the Governor's house at Nathiagalli, over Miranjani to Thandiani. Other enthusiasts take the trail through pastoral meadow and forest to the top of 9,234-foot-high Mukshpuri, one of the highest peaks hereabouts.

The road from the Gallis to Murree winds and twists through the dappled shadows and glades of mountain forest, past foaming rivers with rock-filled pools and water-mills, and the Ayubia National Park, named after former President Ayub Khan; and on into Khaira Galli and Barian. Everywhere small glades and clearings make ideal picnic spots. One of the loveliest is Bhurban where, as well as picnickers, a nine-hole golf course lures many summer *aficionados* of the game.

Way back in the middle of the last century these hill resorts were untouched, the sylvan setting of a rural culture unchanged for centuries, the ancestral home of the Dhund tribe of Punjabis. They claim descent from Abbas, an uncle of the Prophet, who gave rise to the Abbasid caliphate of Baghdad. The Dhunds came under Sikh domination in the 1830s.

The first of the Europeans to develop these hills as a summer retreat was James Abbott. Under the British, Murree was the summer capital of the Punjab for a quarter of a century before its transfer to Simla. Now more than a century later, snowbound in winter, pleasantly cool in summer, as evidence

Opposite: Inscribed on the slopes of a ridgeback above the tree-shaded military cantonment of Abbottabad, the words 'Home of Piffers' bespeak the pride of one of the subcontinent's oldest and most renowned regiments.

of its tremendous popularity, so crowded is Murree in summer that you need a permit to drive your car in the centre of town.

The forested hills on which the town sprawls are crowded with rest houses, guest houses, summer houses, and older buildings of tin and timber — Primrose Cottage, Woodland Walk, *et al* — that reflect the British era in the subcontinent.

Until Independence it was the home of the Murree Brewery, now relocated in Rawalpindi, whose buildings and equipment were destroyed during riots in 1947. Set at more than 7,000 feet above sea level, Murree takes its name from a local word, *Co-marhi*, meaning simply 'high place'.

Abbottabad is also an ideal base from which to explore the hill ranges to its west, along a twisting road through lovely wooded valleys, to Sherwan, perched on a 5,000-foot-high ridge, and beyond.

North of Abbottabad, in the centre of a verdant bowl of farmland, emerald green in spring against the distant backdrop of snowclad mountains and nostalgically mellow in the fall, as the leaves turn to gold and russet, lies Manshera, capital of the district to which it gives its name. Where the Karakoram Highway veers west to bypass the town it cuts through three rocks on either side of the road.

Although eroded and weathered by more than two thousand years, the faint outlines of the inscriptions carved on them in Karoshthi, the local Gandharian dialect, can still be made out, if dimly. In that far distant, sunlit past, the great Mauryan Emperor Ashoka paused at this crossroads of two major trade routes of the subcontinent, from Kashmir and China, to inscribe edicts that have stood testament to time and the ravages of man and weather.

Perhaps the greatest of all those who have ruled India — he held virtually the whole subcontinent under his firm but patriarchal hand for more than forty years — Ashoka, who reigned from 272 to 231 BC, ordered that his edicts should be inscribed on rocks and pillars throughout his empire. In fact, these edicts were proclamation of his government policies.

Tolerant of all beliefs, later in his reign Ashoka became a devout Buddhist and espoused the philosophy of kindness to all living creatures. Indeed, one of his major edicts may well have been the first conservation law ever written. Echoing the Buddha's edict to 'embrace all living things as a mother cares for her son, her only son', his Fifth Pillar Proclamation gave protection to bats, monkeys, rhinoceroses, porcupines, tree squirrels, and the forests in which they lived.

But the edicts that remain in two places in Pakistan — at Manshera and at Shahbaz Garhi on the Peshawar plains — confessed the Emperor's shame at the slaughter involved in his conquest of Kalinga in eastern India and stated that the only way to conquer was through 'righteousness and dharma'; that his duty was always to avail himself to the people to hear their petitions.

In others, he counselled his people to give alms to the priests and the poor;

tolerate all religions; love and honour parents, relatives, and friends; build hospitals for both humans and animals; and plant medicinal herbs so that there would be no shortage of tonics.

Though barely discernible, these priceless legacies of so long ago, now covered by roofing to protect their ancient wisdom as a future heritage, form the focal theme of a public park built in 1988. Close by, a path leads to the summit of Bareri Hill, for centuries a sacred place of Hindu pilgrimage.

North-west lie the beautiful Black Mountains, and at Oghi there's a fort commemorating the frustration of British troops in their attempt to subdue the hill people who played hit-and-run from their mountain strongholds. Every so often a punitive expedition would sally forth from the fort to pillage villages, raze crops, take hostages, and impose fines. But nothing quelled the partisan and fiercely-independent tribesmen, rousing the wrath of early twentieth-century editorialists, 'The tribes obviously need a lesson . . . this behaviour is not to be tolerated.'

To the north-east, hidden in a forested, cup-shaped valley beneath the snows of 16,219-foot-high Bhogarmang, stands the hill-town of Daddar, famous as a health resort for tuberculosis patients. The fresh, invigorating alpine air is beneficial balm for the sufferers, who stay in a sanatorium, and the grandeur of the landscapes a soothing salve for the eyes.

But Daddar is simply a promise of what follows. For this is the threshold to what many believe is arguably the most beautiful of all Pakistan's northern vistas: the unspoilt and changeless Kaghan Valley, reached these days at the end of an exhilarating but none-too-strenuous three-day trek along a trail through the Bhogarmang valley and over the Sharan pass.

Some, however, still prefer to take the old Mughal road from Manshera which cuts over the pine-crested Batrasi Ridge and across the River Kunhar to Balakot, gateway to Kaghan Valley.

Although the Mughals always marched on to their beloved Vale of Kashmir, many argue that Kaghan is fairer still. More than 160 kilometres long, the valley traces the course of the River Kunhar from a height of around 3,000 feet in the south to the Babusar Pass in the north — once the only road to Gilgit and the Roof of the World — where, at more than 13,600 feet, the trail leads over the ridge and down to Chilas.

Great forests roll down its steeply sloping walls, and glistening jade lakes, interspersed with meadows, cling like jewelled clasps to its floor beneath the shadows of the mountain ridges above. Sylvan Kaghan Valley bestows the bounty of its beauty on all who behold it. But there are perils, too — slick and treacherous glacier tails that cross the jeep road, and occasional landslides that rumble down the slopes at its northern end.

Yet, so gladdening to the eye is the valley, little will deter the first-time visitor in pursuit of its little by-trails and side valleys. Late spring, midsummer, and fall are the most attractive seasons in which to enjoy the

Opposite: Snowclad 17,325-feet-high Malika Parbat, with its attendant Musa-ka-Musalla — 'the prayer mat of Moses' — dominates the horizon above Kaghan Valley's upper reaches.

Kaghan Valley's delights, although the Babusar Pass is open only briefly during the high summer months.

The valley proper begins after the dry and dusty town of Balakot, locale of a fierce nineteenth-century battle between the forces of a Muslim warrior, Ahmed Shah Brewli — killed in 1831— and Ranjit Singh's armies. His green-tiled mausoleum stands on the banks of the Kunhar. Twenty-one years later, James Abbott despatched a force to the valley to put down a rebellion among Kaghan's Saiad community that had been inspired by one of Ahmed's disciples. The expeditionary force met no opposition. But although the Saiads surrendered without fighting, they were expelled from their homeland to live in exile for three years on the plains around Manshera.

Twenty-four kilometres up the valley from Balakot, high on a precipitous eastern shoulder of Kaghan, stands the town of Kawai where a side trail leads through dense forest along a muddy and rutted lumber track to emerge on the rim of perhaps the loveliest plateau overlooking the valley, 7,750-foot-high Shogran.

Above: Alpine wildlife of the Pakistan mountains includes blue sheep, Marco Polo sheep, ibex, and the rare snow leopard.

Stirring in the fitful May breeze, flowers bend and nod in the green meadows beneath 12,744-foot-high Makra while, a few miles to the north, massive and majestic within the narrow, constraining perspective and pellucid air of the valley, you feel you could reach out and touch the mass of 17,356-foot-high Malika Parbat thrusting its ice spires into the blue sky. Nearby, its minions, Makra and Musa-ka-Musalla — the 'prayer mat of Moses' — bow their heads in deference to the largest of the valley's peaks.

These meadows, and those above, are the summer pastures of the nomadic Gujar pastoralists. Independent and hardy, the Gujar women wear vivid, gaily-coloured dresses that reflect the pastel brilliance of the wild flower meadows.

West of Shogran, on the opposite plateau, stands one of Pakistan's most precious indigenous hardwood forests, rich in the abundance of its bird life, with tranquil walks leading to idyllic views at the edge of escarpments and ridges.

The farther north you travel along the valley, climbing steadily all the while, the wilder and more remote it becomes, instilling a sense of time removed. Roaming this peaceful wilderness, privileged intruder into another world, the pressures of city life swiftly fade.

Gem of gems in this treasury of natural jewels is Saiful Muluk, at the head of an eastern side valley ten kilometres from Naran village, and its sister lakes, Lulusar (at the foot of the Babusar Pass where the Kunhar launches its journey to the Jhelum and the Indus) and Dudupatsar.

Floating limpid on the startlingly blue waters of the one-kilometre-long lake is the mirror image of Malika Parbat at whose base — at 10,500 feet — lies Saiful Muluk. Frozen over in winter, in early spring the surface, reflecting its ring of ice-encrusted guardian peaks, is dotted with tiny islands of ice. In

April and May the meadows on the lake shores become a riot of colourful wild flowers.

Lie here in the balm of a hazy summer day, amid the quiet and the hum of insects at work, and ponder the lake's name — taken from Prince Saiful Muluk, who fell in love with a lake nymph. So enamoured of her was he that one day he snatched away her clothing to gaze upon her beauty. To save her modesty, the nymph promised to wed the prince.

As they rode away into the sunset to live happily ever after, the nymph's demon lover was so incensed that he flooded the whole of the Kaghan Valley.

And, says local folklore, fairies, demons, and nymphs still live in the waters of Saiful Muluk, to revel at night on its grassy shores. Woe to those who encounter these mythical folk.

Back in the main valley, the road now begins to narrow as it climbs through the mountain pastures to the treeless slopes around the village of Besal and beyond — to the dramatic and forbidding Babusar Pass; a road so neglected that even for the most adventurous it's a hair-raising journey.

Few indeed attempt it, but many do travel as far as Besal to gaze upon the font of the Khunar; the lake that so delighted whimsical Irish writer Dervia Murphy when she cycled from Ireland to India — even over the Babusar Pass.

She wrote of this one-kilometre-wide jade jewel at the throat of the Kaghan where its surface reflects the craggy blue-grey mountains and glaciers around it:

*The water was clear but dark green and one of the loveliest sights of my life was the perfect reflection of the white snow in the depth of that greenness.*

She found the shores littered with the ice detritus of Kaghan's melting glaciers before pressing on, carrying the bicycle that was supposed to carry her, over the Babusar.

Back in Manshera, the Karakoram Highway also beckons the adventurer forward, through rocky gorge and between china clay cliffs, over circles of fertile valleys with panoramas of the Black Mountains westward, to Batgram and beyond. Veering north-west, the road sinks slowly down through avenues of poplar trees to where the Indus valley narrows beneath the slopes of Pir Sar on the river's western banks, and then, near Thakot, you'll get your first glimpse of this raging torrent that rushes on to become a river of history that waters a nation of more than 100 million people.

For many years Pir Sar was believed to be Aornos, the mountain peak that echoes in the history of Alexander the Great, and one signboard by the road proclaims it as such. But Alexander and his armies never travelled this far.

Thakot is the official start of the Karakoram Highway. As you cross a splendid suspension bridge, its twin towers at either side fittingly crowned, a sign welcomes travellers to the KKH before they travel briefly through Swat

Opposite: Child of the valleys
— a Kohistani youngster
fetching water.

to Besham, gateway to remote and still mysterious Kohistan. There's a monument with a Qur'anic inscription on the northern side of the bridge, above the river rapids, that commemorates the memory of those who died building the KKH:

*All those who have laid down their lives in the path of God, do not call them dead. They are alive but you are not aware.*

This region marks the transition from the horizontal to the vertical perspectives of northern Pakistan. Suddenly, almost claustrophobically, the walls of the Indus gorge close in — in some places so narrow that the cliffs of raddled rock, veined and seamed by weather and erosion, seem to exclude the light. Sometimes the gorge seems as if it is about to fall inwards.

At other corners, as they march higher and higher into the sky, the tops of the peaks are dusted with snow. Great buttresses emerge hundreds of feet above the sheer drop to the Indus, foaming over its bed of pebbles and giant boulders, hurled down in one of the many and frequent cataclysms that shudder through The Roof of the World.

Covering an area of roughly 9,000 square kilometres, Kohistan is one of the highest regions in the world. It consists almost entirely of dauntingly rugged mountains, many above 15,000 feet high, that sandwich tiny, fertile valleys laced together only by a few rough trails. Cultivating their staple, maize, in the arid, stony terraces that pitch down the seemingly vertical mountainsides, villagers eke out a meagre existence.

Many of these villages are fortified strongholds designed to deter enemies and protect crops. For centuries Kohistan was the subcontinent's equivalent of America's Wild West — a land called Yaghistan, which means the land of the outlaw, or savage. Few ventured over the passes into its mountain barriers, for here lived runaways, villains, vagabonds, and outcasts from more stable societies.

Yet Besham, standing on the banks of the Indus, boasts its share of alpine beauty, especially in summer when the river is in spate. It's here that the old Silk Route veered westward, over the Shangla Pass with its magnificent panoramas and vistas, to cross into Swat.

The fourth-century Chinese Buddhist pilgrim Fa Hien found the Silk Route spectacularly hair-raising. Describing his feelings at the edge of a precipice he wrote:

*When one approached the edge of it, his eyes became unsteady; and if he wished to go forward in the same direction there was no place on which he could place his foot. . . . In former times men had chiselled paths along the rocks and distributed ladders on the face of them, to the number altogether of 700, at the bottom of which there was a suspension bridge of ropes, by which the river was crossed, its banks being there eighty paces apart.*

Above: Spring blossom in a mountain valley.

Opposite: Cutting between the cleft of two high points, less than a century ago 13,600-feet-high Babusar Pass, on the old 'Silk Road', was the only way through the almost impenetrable mountain barrier of the Pamir Knot that divides China from the north-west of the subcontinent.

He may well have been speaking of the Indus gorge beyond Besham where the highway has been carved along a contour of the mountains that is sometimes 1,300 feet above the boiling, white water rapids below. One of the few settlements on this section of the highway is Dubair, notable for the bazaar that lines the road and the fine-boned, aquiline faces of the rifle-toting Kohistani tribesmen.

Because of the highway, one of Kohistan's many beautiful valleys, Chowa Dara, is easily accessible. Some thirty-five kilometres beyond Besham, this green and forested fifteen-kilometre-long valley stands above a small reservoir perched atop a hill.

Once a chain of volcanic islands in the Tethys Sea, floating on a small oceanic geological raft, Kohistan is in the centre of the colliding continents. It is trapped and inexorably crushed between the two great continental plates and carried relentlessly northward by the momentum of the Indian plate as it grinds into the Asian plate at the reckless speed, geologically speaking, of about five centimetres a year.

In December 1974 unstoppable India met immovable Asia. It was a nudge like no other. As Ernest Hemingway once observed, the earth moved. Kohistan literally jumped in the air. Its main town, Patan on the Karakoram Highway, and the valley in which it lies, were virtually obliterated. Whole mountainsides came crashing down, taking shepherds and farmers with them.

It happened just seconds after hundreds of Chinese workers had knocked off work and gone to their tents. Massive rock slides poured down, wiping out a new stretch of the Karakoram Highway but miraculously the Chinese escaped. Yet when the dust settled, 5,000 of Kohistan's tiny population were dead and 15,000 injured. And, although relief poured in from around the world, rescue and rehabilitation work, compounded by the difficult terrain and lack of communications, was long and arduous.

Raised by the roadside as you enter Patan is another inscribed memorial to those who died building the Karakoram Highway:

*Sometime in the future when others will ply the KKH little will they realize the amount of sweat, courage, dedication, endurance and human sacrifice that has gone into the making of this road. But as you drive along, tarry a little to say a short prayer for those silent brave men of the Pakistan Army who gave their lives to realize a dream, now known as the Karakoram Highway. We pioneered the mighty Karakoram and carved a road with blood.*

In the years since 1974, Patan has been much rebuilt and little remains to indicate the immensity of the disaster that struck this small community. Solid new granite buildings have replaced those that were torn away where the town struggles down the slopes of a delightful but isolated valley.

It's when you reach these small settlements that you suddenly realize the

sense of isolation, sometimes desolation, that pervades the subconscious in these remote regions.

Teeming Karachi, at the southern end of the subcontinent, lies 1,850 kilometres away, Beijing, to the north and then east, is more than 5,400 kilometres distant, and the central Asian city of Kashgar is 1,050 kilometres away. Today you can drive easily between them. But in a tree-shaded garden above a babbling brook in the Kayal Valley, just beyond Patan, they seem as remote and distant as the moon.

Now, for some distance, the highway travels through sheer cliffs that rise impossibly high above the shadowed road. You feel you can almost reach out and touch the other side of the gorge, but it's only an illusion.

This section of the highway claimed the lives of more men than any other. As the road, actually blasted out of the mountainside, cuts into the cliff, 1,200 feet above the river, you may ask yourself what sustains such faith in the power of the rock overhead to suspend itself indefinitely with such a mass of weight pushing down on it — and, more important, what sustains the faith of those who pass beneath?

Even today this section remains the most hazardous. An average of at least one vehicle a month plunges down the sheer cliff to the river — either through mechanical failure or the driver's reckless folly.

The damage caused by mud and rock falls and earth movement is also greater than on any other sector — and members of the Pakistan Army's Frontier Works Organisation still lay down their lives in the struggle to maintain the highway and keep it open.

Then, just before Sazin, the mountains fall away from the road as the gorge widens out into a sandy valley and the river meanders briefly through the broad plain. In the swirling waters, villagers check their wicker fishtraps and nets.

Ahead lies the Pamir Knot — and westward the lost and lovely horizons that were created when two continents first clashed.

# 3 Lost and

# Lovely Horizons

Step by step, out of the barren brown hills of Afghanistan, the mountains of the Hindu Kush march into Pakistan — the valleys between each of the ridges forming necklaces of green oases sustained by the grey snow-fed rivers that rush down their slopes. Yet always the trace of the deserts far below in Afghanistan pervades the tiny villages where ragged columns of smoke from the cooking fires rise in the thin mountain air.

All seems sere aridity. Yet within this wilderness lie some of the most beautiful mountain valleys found anywhere, and which, until recently, formed the physical boundaries of two fabled kingdoms.

Among the first Europeans to discover the delights of these scenic wonderlands was Alexander the Great. In 327 BC, after striding east through the Khyber Pass and the ancient frontier town of Peshawar, the Macedonian King glanced to the north, where the gentle folds of the green foothills that form the lower flank of the southern bastion of the Hindu Kush begin to rise up out of the plains. There was an allure, a promise about them, strong enough to divert him from his advance on the Punjab.

Dividing his 50,000-strong army, he turned northward with one half — leaving the other half to march on to Gandhara — crossing the Kabul River above its confluence with the Indus, somewhere around what is now Nowshera, the military town established two centuries ago by the British, to climb the Malakand Pass which rises to almost 5,000 feet.

Guarding the magic valley of Swat, the pass lies beyond the town of Mardan, another military town established roughly two centuries ago by the British, and the original home of Pakistan's crack Frontier Force Regiment which began as the Corps of Guides in 1846. A memorial arch in the town's centre commemorates the Regiment's proud tradition of valour:

*. . . The annals of no army and no regiment can show a brighter record of devoted bravery than has been achieved by this small band of guides. By their deeds they have conferred undying honour not only to the regiment to which they belong, but on the whole British army.*

It's a tradition of courage that inspired Charles Miller's best-selling *Khyber* and stirred the pages of M. M. Kaye's *The Far Pavilions*.

Twisting and turning in a series of steep hairpin bends, a dizzying sheer drop of a thousand feet or more, now this side, now the other, the precipitous single-lane road climbs ever upward until, at a place just before it crests the summit, it presents a breathtaking view of the Swat Valley's southern reaches.

Far below, a tapestry of vivid emerald rice paddies and terraced fruit orchards on the hillsides — ablaze with blossoms of white, pink, yellow, and

Previous pages: Ferrymen ply the broad meanders of the Swat River in a traditional raft kept afloat by inflated oxhides.

red — greets the eye. Above, the sun melts the azure sky into a delicate haze, the light soft and soothing.

No wonder Swat is known as 'The Switzerland of Pakistan'. Truly, as Pathan poet Khushal Khan Khattak wrote, it's a land 'meant to give kings gladness'.

For thousands of years men have coveted this hidden pearl in the bosom of the great mountains. It's beauty is stained with the blood of envy and avarice. As recently as the end of the last century, men were still fighting for possession of this lustrous jewel.

It embraces all the great epochs of invasion and religion that have influenced the subcontinent. Indeed, so much did it delight the King of Macedon, Alexander the Great, that he fought four major battles to make it part of his empire. So did those who came in the millenniums before and after him. Indeed, Swat's human history is rooted hundreds of centuries ago in the Stone Age.

Thousands of years later, in 1700 BC, the first invaders, the Aryans, crossed over into Swat from central Asia, descendants of the Hindu believers who composed the Rig-Veda, the oldest surviving religious text in the world with 1,208 Hindu poems. One of the vedas that exist from this era tells of victory won on the banks of the Suvastu, now the Swat.

Interwoven for more than a millennium with the spread of Buddhism, the Hindus remained in Swat until the first century of this millennium and left a priceless legacy of architecture, monuments, and scholarship.

Much later, in the mid-nineteenth century, this princely state, that can surely lay claim to be a *Shangri-la*, came to be dominated by the Akhund of Swat and was ruled over by his successors until as recently as 1969.

As the Wali of Swat, a title bestowed by the British in 1926, Prince Miangul Abdul Wadud built a network of good roads throughout the valley and on the mountain slopes. Picturesque rest houses in the pine and conifer forests now offer shelter for anglers testing their skills against the plump trout in the well-stocked streams that chuckle over the rocks and cascade down the falls. Farmhouses perch on precipitous slopes above terraced fields where the alpine air is crisp and bracing — like a charge of champagne.

As you begin the descent to the valley floor, the ring of sword on shield echoes in the mind. The top of the Malakand pass is guarded by a fort famous for its garrison of 1,000 Sikh infantry. In 1897, under British officers, these troops heroically defied an army of 10,000 Pukhtun Swats, who had worked themselves into a religious frenzy for eight days before attacking under the command of the so-called Mad Mullah. Almost 4,000 of the Mullah's zealots died in the greatest pitched battle ever fought by the British in the North-

Opposite: Wherever you go in remote and lovely Chitral the horizon is dominated by the compelling panorama of 25,230-feet-high Tirich Mir, highest point of the Hindu Kush, westernmost bastion of the Roof of The World.

The fort overlooks an older Hindu Shahi fort above Bat Khela, a market town that marks the descent to the valley floor. Where you enter the valley, the waters of the Swat River, which nourish this other Eden, have spent their rage and eddy through broad meanders.

Bearded Pukhtun warriors, like patriarchs from an Old Testament lithograph, women clad in the all-embracing Islamic shawl, *sadar*, and ragged urchins, work the rich black soil of the paddies and grain fields with rhythmic economy bending and planting, hoeing and digging. Fine-featured, olive-skinned, with black hair and brown eyes, they look strikingly alike. All the young lads wear slingshots around their neck, ever ready for miniature feudal war with the youngsters of another family.

Irrigation canals criss-cross the land. Huge water buffalo with sweptback horns wallow in ponds and pools. By the roadside tea houses at frequent intervals offer refreshing cups of sweet, milky tea ladled out of huge, black-stained kettles.

In the spartan, stonewall, flat-roofed houses of the villages, cattle dung fires in the middle of the kitchen floor send smoke eddying around the house before it escapes through a hole in the roof. And though taxis and cars are increasing in numbers, the donkey and the mule remain the universal beasts of burden.

Despite the natural beauty all around, life in these quaint and timeless villages can be harsh and unrewarding. During summer it's hot, muggy, and unpredictable, with temperatures often more than 100°F (38°C). At the extreme edge of the monsoon belt, the valley frequently suffers devastating droughts and freak storms that wipe out entire crops. But the weather is extremely local, too: while there is a violent storm in one place, only two or three kilometres away the sun shines brightly.

Thus farming remains a gamble. Only fifteen per cent of the land is arable, providing just fractions of an acre for each person. More than half is deforested rangeland, good only for grazing. Another twenty per cent is virgin forest rapidly coming under the axe, causing erosion and denuding the land. At least ten per cent is unusable riverbed and glacier.

But in the good years it holds its promise as a land of milk and honey. Given sufficient rain, double cropping is possible and farmers can reap wheat and clover in the spring, rice and maize in the autumn. Now orange groves blossom in the valley's fertile South, and crops like tomatoes and potatoes have been introduced.

Most of the people — the population doubled in the fifty years from 1930 and has been swollen still more by the tide of refugees from Afghanistan —

live along the watershed of the Swat River. But a steady stream of migrants to the southern cities in search of work has averted the threat of a population and food crisis.

Nearly all are Pukhtun — that race of fearless and fearsome warriors of the North-West Frontier whose code of honour, *Pukhtunwali*, is based on three principles: revenge, hospitality, and refuge; *badal*, *melmastia*, and *nanawatia*. These also embrace the virtues of equality, respect, loyalty, pride, bravery, purdah (women's exclusion), the pursuit of romantic encounters, Islam, and selfless love for a friend.

Though Pukhtun hospitality knows no bounds and none can refuse refuge of those who seek it, for those not steeped in Pukhtun traditions it seems a cruel and traumatic society, a daily round of acrimonious conflict.

In Swat, unlike other Pukhtun communities, this is notably between individuals — not groups. 'Instead,' writes Charles Lindholm in *Generosity and Jealousy,* 'lone men struggle against their closest patrilineal relatives in personal, perpetual and sometimes deadly competition over the land of their common grandfather.' It is, he notes, the vital matters of revenge and warfare that dominate life in Swat — even inside the family.

Husband and wife, it seems, are locked in a continuous struggle for power. Husbands seek to subdue their wives and, failing that, to humiliate them, perhaps by taking a second wife. The wife responds through open fighting and perhaps the use of magic spells against her rivals. Some resort to poisoning their husbands.

Men, notes Lindholm, are allowed — 'and encouraged' — to beat their wives regularly. Only if bones are broken may she run away, and even then tradition says she must return. Kith and kin of a shameful or shameless wife can take their own revenge by shooting her. In this instance, it is doubtful if anyone will wish to quarrel with Lindholm's observation that 'married life in Swat is fraught with tensions'.

But, ever-friendly to strangers, hospitable to the point of what seems certifiable insanity, and incapable of speaking a lie, there's something magnificent about Pukhtun men. Disdainful of wheedling and toadying, Pukhtuns do not make good traders. To shame troublesome customers they prefer to give them what they want. Not, indeed, as Lindholm observes, a profitable way to run a store.

A favourite proverb to a favourite son says, 'The eye of the dove is lovely, my son, but the sky is made for the hawk. So cover your dove-like eyes and grow claws.' Sons are circumcised in the tradition of Islam, usually before they reach the age of seven. Once an occasion for feasting and dancing second only to a wedding, these days the operation is performed painlessly and

Opposite: Young Pukhtun boy with wicker-framed fish net in Swat Valley.

quietly at the local health clinic, or by the nearest doctor.

Even so, in such deep-rooted societies change is slow. Thus, though linked to Pakistan by road and regular air services, the valley remains much as it has over the centuries. Encircled by its mountains and hills, it dreams on — an echo of the past that evokes a feeling of eternity.

The first people to occupy the valley built stone houses and developed a slow-moving wheel on which to spin and fashion grey and black pottery. Under their care, using primitive implements of stone and wood to prepare the soil, the fallow land burgeoned with grains and fruits. They tended cattle too, and sheep and goats.

Metal — copper and gold — was shaped as jewellery. But as their social structures developed, so did their gift for innovation. Later generations used weapons and tools of iron: knives, hoes, sheep shears, and needles. In Swat, some of the most distant past has survived the centuries.

The valley plains are dotted with many graveyards, some of which have been in constant use by the people of Swat for 3,000 years or more. Archaeologists who excavated Aryan graves discovered that the corpses had been partly cremated and their graves lined and sealed with large stone slabs. The dead were left with pots and pans and other artefacts of daily use.

All along the valley, Swat's long history of Hindu civilization is commemorated by rock carvings and ancient forts. Swat is rich in the treasures of its other previous cultures, too. Buddhist stupas, monasteries, and rock carvings abound.

The valley road levels out just beyond Bat Khela at Chakdara, a seat of trade and commerce for more than 3,000 years. History shrouds Chakdara — from the misty aeons of so long ago right up to the present day. For centuries the tramp of the invader's boot has echoed through this bazaar that lies on one of the great ancient silk routes between China and central Asia, crossing into Afghanistan through the Nawa Pass.

On the nearby hilltops glower the brooding ruins of the fortresses built between the eighth and tenth centuries by the Hindu Shahi — Turkish Kings. Walk up Damkot Hill overlooking the town to see the neatly excavated ruins of one the largest — razed by fire on the orders of Mahmud of Ghazni, first of the Islamic conquerors around the end of the tenth century. It is a panorama that delighted not only Mahmud but the Mughal Emperor, Akbar the Great.

In the sixteenth century, Akbar built a massive fort at the base of Damkot Hill to guard his vital trade route below. Over its ruins, 300 years later in 1896, the British built another that is now a citadel of Pakistan's modern army. It's on the actual summit of the hill, however — where there's a small observation post called Churchill's Picket — that the Hindu kings built their

Right: Ruins of one of the greatest of the Buddhist cities, Butkara in Swat Valley.

Right: Traditional ferry of the Swat Valley — a frame of sticks above inflated ox hides.

Opposite: Goats cross a
wooden bridge in Upper Swat
valley.

fortress.

As ever, 'like most young fools looking for trouble' more than just an
observer, Churchill, a £5-a-column war correspondent for the London *Daily
Telegraph,* was a participant ('I wore my long Cavalry sword well sharpened')
in the thick of one of the most recent battles at this very spot, when the feared
and indomitable Pathan tribesmen rose up in anger against their British
overlords in 1897.

*There was a ragged volley from the rocks; shouts, exclamations, and a scream.
One man was shot through the breast and pouring with blood; another lay on
his back kicking and twisting. The British officer was spinning round just
behind me, his face a mass of blood, his right eye cut out. Yes, it was certainly
an adventure.*
*It is a point of honour on the Indian frontier not to leave wounded men
behind. Death by inches and hideous mutilation are the invariable measure
meted out to all who fall in battle into the hands of the Pathan.*

Now stand here on the summit, as did Alexander, Akbar, and Churchill,
and see the glories of the valley crowned in the far distance by the great
snowclad pyramids of the Hindu Kush and you'll need no more convincing
why men have fought for the treasures of Swat.

From this vantage point, in one sweep the eye takes in all the passes into the
lower reaches of the Swat. To the west, Malakand. To the south, Shah Kot and
Mora. To the east, Barikot. And below, and to the north, the great trade route.

For nigh on 4,000 years armies have contended possession of this strategic
summit. Centuries ago, after the Aryans abandoned this location, monks of a
first-century AD Buddhist community resettled it. Buddhism flourished in
Swat for many centuries.

Born in 540 BC, Siddhartha Gautama Buddha was the son of King
Suddhodhan. A Royal Prince, Buddha wanted for nothing as he grew up at
his palace home at Taulihawa, about twenty-four kilometres from Lumbini,
in what is now Nepal. At the time of his birth, Brahminism was the dominant
faith in India and there was great poverty and hardship among the people.
But Buddha grew to manhood unaware of the people's suffering. When he
discovered it he became an ascetic, roaming the Indian countryside close to
death most of the time from self-deprivation.

Finally, he abandoned his wandering way of life and became reclusive,
meditating on life until, under a pipal tree at Gaya near Benares, India, he
evolved the philosophy that would sustain millions through the next 2,500
years and out of which came his name, 'Enlightened One' — the Buddha.

The way, he said, was to reject extremes of pleasure or pain and follow an

'Eightfold Path' based on 'Four Noble Truths'. Mankind suffered, pronounced the Buddha, because of its attachment to people and possessions. In a world where nothing is permanent, desire and suffering could be banished by an attachment to rightfulness.

The individual, he theorized, was simply an illusion created by the chain of cause and effect — *karma* — and trapped in the cycle of incarnation and reincarnation. *Nirvana*, the highest point of pure thought, could only be attained by the extinction of self — and the abolition of *karma*.

For forty-five years, the Buddha preached his doctrine before attaining *nirvana* when he died at the age of eighty. Thus Swat Valley became part of northern Pakistan's great Gandharan Buddhist civilization.

A collection of boulders at the western base of Damkot is carved with figures that depict, among others, the slim, robe-clad person of Padmapani, the lotus bearer Bodhisattva. Atop the 3,900-foot-high summit they built a stupa — a dome-shaped mound representing the way to *nirvana* — and monastery. It was a community of peace and meditation that survived more than 400 years before falling to the sword of the Hindu rajputs.

Indeed, Chakdara is the centre of one of the richest and most outstanding repositories of Buddhist art and culture found anywhere in the world. Many Gandharan Buddhist sculptures in Chakdara Museum's renowned collection were recovered from the ruins of the many monasteries in the region, some still to be excavated. But one, at the base of the Malakand Pass, was destroyed when engineers blasted the hillside to build a canal tunnel.

At Chat Pat on the Dir road, another monastery, nestling in a fold in the gentle hills, overlooking a small and peaceful valley, was buried in a landslide. It was built late in the first century and developed during the next three centuries.

Excavations uncovered a treasury of Gandhara art that decorated its many stupas and temples. These sophisticated metal sculptures were carved by Bactrian artists imported from north Afghanistan by the Kushans. There's a marked deterioration in quality between the early, original Bactrian carvings, and those sculpted later by artists of local origin.

Some little distance away, at Andan Dheri, an immense number of similar treasures — more than 500 along with many coins of the Kushana period — were discovered during excavations of what was probably the most important Buddhist centre in the region. The stupas and the monastery which stood here marked the spot where Buddha, it was said, in an incarnation as Indra, transformed himself during one of India's great famines into a giant snake that lay dead as the starving cut the flesh to feed themselves. As it was cut, each piece of flesh miraculously renewed itself, thus curing the hungry and the sick.

The stupa beside the monastery stood eighty feet high. Built in the late first century, the main stupa, fourteen votive stupas, and the monastery were in use until the seventh century. But now much of the site is under the plough.

A few kilometres south-west of Andan Dheri, guarded at its narrowest point by the ruins of the massive eighth-century Hindu bastion of Kat Kala — 'Fort of the Pass' — is the lovely Talash Valley, lined with one unexplored, unexcavated stupa and monastery after another.

Yet Kat Kala is best remembered as the possible location of Massaga, scene of an epic battle between Alexander's 25,000 troops and the Assakenoi. Terrified by the war engines, mobile towers, and rock-hurling catapults that the Macedonian army had dragged through the rugged mountains, the Assakenoi's 30,000 foot soldiers, 2,000 cavalry, and thirty elephant were locked in mortal combat with the invaders for four bloody days before capitulating.

According to the first-century historian, Curtius, the humiliated defenders then despatched envoys to plead mercy from Alexander. When it was granted, the Queen of Massaga brought the Macedonian gifts and libations of wine in golden bowls. Placing her baby son at Alexander's feet, the Queen was allowed to remain ruler. 'Some have believed this indulgent treatment,' wrote Curtius, 'was accorded rather to the charms of her person than to pity for her misfortunes.' At any rate, she later gave birth to another son, whom she named Alexander.

Some forty kilometres beyond Kat Kala is Balamabat, one of the oldest human settlements in the Swat Valley. It has been in continuous occupation, by Aryans, Buddhists, Hindus, and Muslims, since 1500 BC. It's also been extensively excavated, uncovering the ruins of houses built 2,500 years ago and the altars of fire worshippers, whose pagan rites are echoed even today by the burning of juniper on fire stands by pagan priestesses.

Thick stands of juniper mould the contours of the hills around Balamabat with a sturdy tracery of green limbs. Ever in the background, above the ridges and valleys, stand the snowy-crested mountains, foreshortening perspectives in a breathtaking panorama.

But those who wander this far off course in Swat either continue north-west to Dir and Chitral; or return to explore the main reaches of the valley through the gateway town of Landakai, some twelve kilometres beyond Chakdara, where visitors to Swat register their presence in a book kept by the police.

Atop the hills, and in the little dales between the two towns, stand more ruined monasteries and forts. Close to Landakai, the Nimogram valley is unique for its three stupas devoted to Buddha the Teacher, *Dharma*, the

Buddhist doctrine, and *Sangha,* the Buddhist order. There are several votive stupas, too. Nimogram is also noted for some superb sculptures unearthed during excavations, and now housed in the Swat museum in the capital of Saidu Sharif.

To the north, on the main valley road, you'll see the flat mound of Barikot Hill, scene of Alexander the Great's protracted struggle to capture the ancient town of Bazir. Unable to enter Bazir's walls, Alexander left the town besieged and marched eastward along the Swat River to attack the town of Ora.

The Macedonian had ordered one of his lieutenants, Koinos, to set up a garrison strong enough to deter the Bazirans from leaving the city to work their lands and then to march on and rejoin his vanguard. But when Koinos had established the garrison and marched off to rejoin Alexander, the defenders streamed out to cut down the soldiers of the garrison and descend to the plain.

There they ran into the rearguard of Koinos's troops and quickly retreated. But before they reached the safety of Bazir's walls, more than 500 lay dead and seventy were taken prisoner. Soon after, on hearing of the fall of Ora, the disheartened inhabitants abandoned Bazir altogether — fleeing to the rocky peak of Mount Ilam which they called Aornos, to seek protection there among its divine spirits.

Digging in among the big square blocks of rock that mark Ilam's peak — possibly prehistoric altars like those at Stonehenge in Britain — the Bazirans waited for the expected assault. It did not come at once. Ravines, gullies, and fast-flowing streams hindered the advance of the Macedonian army and their bulky and awkward war machines. Engineers took three days to build a ramp across one 1,600-foot-wide ravine. Then the infantry climbed the cliff face and the Bazirans fled, many falling to the sword.

Later, in the eighth century, the Hindu Shahi rulers built a fort on the ruins of Bazir of which one wall, rising fifty feet high, still stands. The rest of the hill crest is under the plough, but the view of the verdant plains below against the backdrop of 9,222-foot-high Mount Ilam, its sacred peak encircled by clouds, justifies the climb.

Mystical and inspiring, Ilam has long been the home of the gods of the local tribes and served as inspiration for the religious mythology of Buddhist, Hindu, and Muslim.

Now, where the wind whispers across the mountaintop, the roar of conflict and bloody battle long stilled, the gods repose again in peace. The Tibetans called it Mount Ilo and the Chinese traveller, Hsuan Tsang, who climbed the mountain in AD 630, identified it as Mount Hilo, the place where the Buddha, in a previous incarnation, sacrificed half his life to hear a few words of

Above: Cultivated flowers of the valleys.

Above: Wildflowers of the mountains at heights of between 14,000 and 16,000 feet where plant life maintains a tenacious grip.

revelation.

The mystics who embraced his doctrine found haven in Swat from the persecution of the marauding Aryans and named the valley *Udyana* — the garden. Later, the Hindus carved the name Sri Ram, one of Vishnu's incarnations, Rama, on Ilam's rocky summit. Until the birth of Pakistan in 1947 it was one of the many Hindu pilgrimage places on the subcontinent — thousands of worshippers trekking up the steep slopes, passing the now-abandoned white palace at Sufaid Mahal which was the summer home of the first Wali of Swat, to pay homage at Vishnu's throne.

Looking south from this impressive viewpoint you'll see the pine-cloaked shoulders of Karakar Pass, 4,384 feet high, which leads into the lovely Buner Valley where Akbar the Great suffered one of his rare defeats. When he stormed the pass in 1586 to invade Swat he lost most of his 8,000-strong army to the defiant defenders.

Nearby, on the road from Barikot to Karakar, you can explore the ruins of one of the best preserved Buddhist shrines in Swat, at Gumbat — a central cell encircled by a processional corridor, surmounted by a fifty-foot-high dome. Several small stupas nearby have become grassy mounds.

But it's beyond Barikot, as you drive towards the Swat capital of Saidu Sharif, that you'll discover some of the most intriguing aspects of the valley's ancient heritage — Aryan and Buddhist rock carvings, the earliest of which date back beyond 1000 BC, and one of Pakistan's many archaeological treasures, the ancient ruined town of Udegram.

Shingerdar, just three kilometres beyond Barikot, is the first of these many wonders of old — a massive and once magnificent golden-domed stupa that's now a crumbling ruin. Plastered and painted with many figures and symbols, the delicate carvings at its base form a frieze commemorating the Buddha's life. In the third and fourth centuries it represented the apogee of Swat's Buddhist cultures.

On a nearby promontory you'll see the vague outline of a rock shaped like an elephant. According to local legend the rock is the metamorphosis of Mata, the white elephant that carried sacred relics of Lord Buddha to this spot for them to be sealed in the golden-domed stupa of the Swat king. Job done, the exhausted elephant fell dead and turned to stone. But it's said the elephant's virtue was rewarded in its next incarnation when it was born a human being though some may argue that this was no reward at all.

Carved on a cliff face beside the stupa, there's a large, much battered relief of Buddha himself. Locals believe — and the heaps of stone at the base testify to the strength of this belief — that there's merit to be won by hurling a rock at the image each time they pass.

It's close to a natural grotto containing the *bas-relief* of a bearded figure, wearing a halo, clad in long coat over Cossack trousers and boots, the traditional costume of Swat's Kushan rulers who held sway in the valley from the first to the third centuries. Lions, flanked by smaller images, support the pedestal on which the image stands.

Now travel another six kilometres and you'll discover rock carvings that go back 3,000 years and beyond, sadly defaced by modern graffiti. There are highly-stylized images of matchstick oxen, ibex, dogs, horses, leopard, other animals, and people in two-wheel chariots. These are the war chariots on which the Aryans rode into Swat about 1700 BC. Above the grotto is a sixth-century AD Buddhist relief, and on another rock nearby, an engraving of Bodhisattva, the Padmani lotus bearer, and attendants.

All this small area is unsurpassed for its wealth of historical treasures. It includes a thriving, modern village — Udegram — close by its walled and castled predecessor, which flourished from 1000 BC until the fourteenth century. The extensive, triangular ruins of the town and its eighth-century Hindu Shahi fort cover twenty different periods, which may explain why the Italian team that excavated the site in the 1950s, although identifying the main area as a bazaar and most of the ruins as shops, left the exhibits unlabelled *in situ*.

The walls extend more than 3,000 feet along the ridge that divides the lower Swat Valley from the upper valley — a battlement that affords inspiring views of both, and the Hindu Kush. The wall encloses a spring that served as the town's water supply — channelled along a series of canals to storage tanks at the foot of the monumental, twenty-foot-wide flight of steps leading up to the citadel, its massive buttresses built from unmortared slate.

Below the citadel a grove of trees marks the shrine of Mahmud of Gazni's local commander, Khushal Khan Baba, who brought the Islamic faith to Swat in the eleventh century when he conquered the local defenders. It is said that this is the spot where he fell while leading the siege of the fortress, held by Raja Gira, the last Hindu ruler.

Close by is Swat's bustling 2,000-year-old 'metropolis' of Mingora with its golf course, hotels, airport, and fascinating bazaar. A thriving trade centre throughout its history, the bazaar reflects the mercantile spirit of its citizens. The bazaar shops and stalls offer a vivid mixture of hand-crafted silver jewellery, semi-precious stones, and colourful woven and embroidered cloths. It's a twin city to the Swat capital of Saidu Sharif, seat of the feudal overlords who ruled the valley from the mid-nineteenth century.

The founder of this dynasty, a wandering Sufi Muslim named Abdul Gaffur, became the Akhund — meaning Messenger of God — of Swat and chose Saidu Sharif, on the banks of the Saidu river, for his capital after uniting the valley's warring factions. In 1863, he and his Pukhtun army fought the British to a standstill in the battle of Ambela Pass.

In honour of this ascetic, charismatic, but warlike leader, Edward Lear, the Victorian humorist and writer of limericks, wrote:

> *Who or why, or which, or what,*
> *Is the Akond of Swat?*
> *Is he tall or short, or dark or fair?*
> *Does he sit on a stool or a sofa or chair, or squat,*
> *The Akond of Swat?*

The Akhund died in 1877. His tomb is close to the palace of his successor, the Wali of Swat, a title which could no doubt have inspired one of Lear's twentieth-century successors to write more doggerel. An astute and ruthless leader who wiped out any possible patrilineal challenge to his title by murdering his first two cousins, Abdul Wadud ruled as the Wali until 1949, when he retired in favour of his son, Feteh Muhammad Khan. The new Wali built the capital's modern hotel to cope with the influx of visitors drawn to Saidu Sharif when tourism burgeoned and his official guest house was unable to accommodate them all.

Two of his daughters married the Pakistan President Ayub Khan, but when, after his downfall, Ayub was given sanctuary in Swat, it was the end of the valley's independence. In 1969 it was taken into Pakistan and the Wali ruled no more. But the palace, set in flowered gardens, remains and, along with the hotel and the Swat Museum — renowned for its collection of Gandharan sculptures and folk history section with exhibits of local wood carvings, embroidery, and tribal jewellery — is one of the capital's major buildings.

All pales, however, besides the peerless Buddhist shrines at Buktara set in the emerald-green fields on the city's outskirts. Though cracked and crumbling, enough has defied the ages to testify to the grandeur that was once Buktara's: an original central stupa built around the second century BC by the Mauryan Emperor Ashoka, and subsequently enlarged five times by building a new stupa on top of the existing one, together with more than 215 votive stupas.

Three of the enlargements took place in the two centuries before the birth of Christ, and by the beginning of the third century AD, under the rule of the Kushanas, Buddhism in Swat was at its apogee: Buktara's stupas had become a place of pilgrimage for worshippers from all over the subcontinent.

Built of soapstone, gilded and painted in bright colours, decorated with elaborate Gandharan statues, and encircled by a pathway set with green, yellow, and blue inlays, the main stupa — said to hold the ashes of Buddha — was a magnificent monument. Crouching lions on tall plinths guarded the approaches to the stupa with its gilded dome covered by stone umbrellas.

Frequently flooded, often damaged by the many earthquakes that characterize this region, Swat's Buddhist devotees constantly restored and redecorated the shrine. When the Gandharan statues were broken, they were replaced with new ones — stucco images of the Buddha's life. Each new layer of plaster added to the stupa was painted with garlands, lotuses, and images of Buddha. Eroded and weathered, broken in many places, some still survive, testament to the strength of one of the world's great religions, including two from the fifth century AD — one of a headless Buddha, another of Buddha standing on a lotus petal.

But in the seventh century, floods so damaged the shrine that it was abandoned for many years. A hundred years or so later, by the time the valley's Buddhists began to build a crude sixth stupa on top of the ruins, the Hindu Shahi rulers had become the new lords of Swat.

And a new cult, one that evolved in this valley, the Tantric Buddhists, had taken sway. Taking its name from a Sanskrit word for weaving, Tantrism reiterates the Buddhist thought literally — all things and all actions are part of a living, constantly changing tapestry — but is opposed to meditation. Devotees express themselves in actual experience and direct action.

Indeed, some Tantric texts suggest that all sin is removed through wine, flesh, fish, women, and sexual congress; and some suggest that sex is not only the ultimate form of bliss and tranquillity — but also wisdom.

This region is rich in archaeological sites. At a place called Buktara II and at Loebanr and Matelai, almost 500 Aryan graves from 1700 BC have been uncovered and, close to Mingora, the ruins of an ancient Aryan town, Aligrama, dating from 1000 BC, now lie bare.

The road out of Mingora marks the final approach to the southernmost buttress of the Hindu Kush on the ascent of the upper Swat Valley. It's carved along a spur that falls sheer into the river. Precipitous, often impassable, it left much of the upper valley isolated during the winter months, preserving a sense of timelessness that still prevails as you twist and turn, moving ever nearer the snow-capped 16,000- and 17,000-foot peaks that mark the end of Swat valley.

Roughly sixteen kilometres beyond Mingora, at the village of Jahanabad, a fourteen-foot-high carving of the Buddha dominates a rock wall in the hillside. It's said that during his travels as the Gautama, he preached a sermon at this spot so moving that a stone stupa — the boulder on which the image is graven — emerged on the place where he stood. Seen as the setting

Opposite: Buddha's image inscribed on a rock face in Swat Valley.

84

sun casts an orange glow across it, the Buddha's untroubled gaze reflects the serenity and tranquillity which is Swat's priceless legacy.

Not that you'd describe nearby Khwazakhela as tranquil. This bustling bazaar is a thriving centre for trade in cloths, fabrics, jewellery, and a flourishing line in instant antiquities — ancient coins just minted, and old wood carvings shaped from the valley's newly-felled timber. So gifted are the town's craftsmen few can detect the false from the real.

You can turn eastward here, if so inclined, and traverse the glorious Shangla Pass that leads over the ridges to Besham and the Indus Valley. But few will be tempted. The greater glories of Swat are still to be discovered.

Already the rivers, fed by the snowmelt and the monsoons, have begun to boil and bubble as they speed along their rocky beds through narrow gorges. In the shallower depths, children fish waist deep with conical-shaped hand nets fastened on an oval frame of wicker and metal. River ferries hereabouts, and lower downstream, are simple rafts of wood that float on inflated ox stomachs and bladders.

Soon these give way to cantilever and suspension bridges and simple but precarious cable cars — small, railed, wooden platforms swinging in the wind as they sway perilously across the deep gorges on a steel suspension cable anchored into the cliff or a convenient tree.

One of the loveliest of Swat's many side valleys is Miandam, roughly fifty-six kilometres from Saidu Sharif, with its village perched at 6,000 feet — cool and refreshing even in hot summer. In the main valley there's also the bazaar town of Madyan, set at more than 4,000 feet, another lodestone of the counterfeiter's art; not just coins and carvings, but stone and stucco Gandharan statues so faithfully recreated that even experts have been fooled.

This aside, the town is a treasury of exquisite shawls — vivid reds, greens, blues, and yellows on black — mentioned in a Sanskrit Buddhist text more than a millennium ago and woven in a nearby valley for more than 2,000 years.

Now the road climbs to Bahrain, another ten kilometres up the valley. Once again you've arrived at a treasure house of local arts and crafts: the superbly-carved doors, balconies, and windows of the older houses testify to centuries of practice and include two beautiful carved wooden mosques, built after the decline of Buddhism and Hinduism.

According to Hsuan Tsang, it was at Bahrain that the dragon rose in springtime. As Hsuan Tsang recounts the town's favourite legend, the dragon — a reincarnation of King Gangi — was so annoyed by the reduction in the size of its tributes from the villages for its services in controlling the rains that it caused too much to fall and the crops were ruined.

So the peasants called on the Buddha to convert the dragon, and when the God of Thunder, Vajrapani, smote the sky and the cliffs, terrifying the dragon into submission, this came about. The dragon was then forbidden to injure the crops. In return, it was granted the harvest once every twelve years.

And so, once every twelve years, the dragon rises and the floods sweep all before them.

The town was the northernmost extent of the Buddhist faith in Swat. Beyond is high country, the road crossing to and fro over the river, twisting and winding along the mountainside through conifer and pine forests that tumble down the mountains, the side in places sometimes plunging sheer almost 500 feet. At one section it emerges from the forest on to a flat spur, curving around a flank at the base of 12,320-foot-high Mount Mankial with a stunning view of its ice-shrouded peak above.

Finally, forty kilometres from Bahrain, at Kalam, it enters an ancient lake bed which has been developed into an alpine tourist resort including chalet-style motel. Here, beneath the magnificent heights of 20,528-foot-high Mount Falaksir, bathed in the luminous pink of the early morning sun, the raging streams of the Utrot and the Ushu sweep through the pine forests to merge as the Swat in a great fork of rock and water.

Westward lies the rich and fertile Utrot Valley and the village of the same name set at 7,300 feet above sea level — a maze of forest and trout streams to delight the alpine lover and trout *aficionados*. But those who wish for really remote, if rugged, tranquillity head north-east up the Ushu Valley. The jeep track rides through dale, glen, and forest to 'The Lake of Fishes', Lake Mahodand, rated by many as the most beautiful trail in the whole of the subcontinent.

For most, however, this is the end of their journey through the Swat Valley. Backpackers, the fit and the hardy, the foolish and the sublime, may all wish to go farther — crossing heights of 12,000 feet or more — over the daunting and often impassable Kachikani Pass and eastward on to Laspur and the Shandur Pass to Gilgit, or west to Mastuj and Chitral.

These involve days of high-altitude trekking over treacherous moraine, scree, and glaciers, far from human contact, in icy temperatures even in summer. A century ago they were the main highways of the remote and inaccessible northern reaches of the region. But even today you travel by foot, jeep, pack beast, or donkey along trails so hair-raising that there are places where a four-wheel drive vehicle has to stop and make a three- or five-point turn to negotiate a crumbling bend hundreds of feet above a raging river: not an exercise for the faint-hearted or vertiginous.

In his 1900 book *The Making of a Frontier*, Colonel Algernon Durand, the

British agent at Gilgit from 1889 to 1894, recalls his march from Gilgit through Shandur Pass:

*Thousands of feet above you are the mountaintops, shattered by frost and sun into the most fantastic outlines, from whose summits fall masses of rock. Below any precipice you consequently see the shingle slope in existence; these slopes sometimes running up thousands of feet at a steep unbroken angle, almost universally of thirty degrees. . . . Whenever there is heavy rain or snow begins to melt in the spring, rock avalanches come down, and I have lain at night for hours listening to the thundering roar of great fragments plunging down from thousands of feet above one's camp.*

The Laspur Pass is less hazardous in places, levelling out in summer on to a greensward plateau with a small lake. That the rewards are worth the effort is not in doubt. But the majority will surely find it easier to retrace their steps down the Swat to Chakdara and take the road from there to Dir — and on to lost and lovely Chitral.

Guarded from time immemorial by the daunting heights of the 10,528-foot-high Lowari Pass in the south and by the massive buttresses of the Hindu Kush to the west, north, and east, the only entrances to Chitral until recently were those high and difficult passes, many of them closed for all but the brief summer months.

Those who chose to drive had to negotiate the seventy kilometres of tortuous hairpin bends and treacherous unstable track over the Lowari Pass between Dir and Drosh. Or take the spectacular but heartstopping and unpredictable fifty-minute flight from Peshawar.

Now engineers of the Pakistan Army's parastatal civil engineering unit, the Frontier Works Organization, have started one of the most stupendous feats of road construction in the world — boring an eighty-two-kilometre-long tunnel beneath the Lowari Pass which, when finished, will open up the marvels of Chitral all the year round.

The valley is at its loveliest in April when it's a riot of fruit blossoms, and in October when the leaves turn to russet. This is wild and wonderful country, the fertile meadows, terraced fields, and orchards of the valley floor verdant contrast to the rugged and forbidding mountains and glaciers. But for much of the winter it is deep in snow.

The first views are breathtaking. In whichever direction you gaze, mountains dominate the horizon. More than 320 kilometres long, set at 5,000 feet above sea level, the valley is encircled by peaks of splendour — rising from 17,750 feet to the highest of the Hindu Kush peaks, 25,290-foot-high Tirich Mir, which appeared to Colonel William Lockhart, one of the first

Europeans to explore this region in the nineteenth century, as 'a mass of frosted silver'.

In the 1980s all visitors were required to register their presence with the police — as much good housekeeping and concern for Chitral's guests as bureaucracy at work. There are many remote and inaccessible side valleys in Chitral in which it is easy to get lost. On many trails, particularly in summer, avalanches and rock slides pose a perennial hazard.

The capital, swollen by the tide of Afghan refugees, boasts a long and dusty bazaar thronged with people and stalls offering local cloth, carpets, stones, jewellery, and the flat hats, distinguished by their rolled-up brims, that all Chitralis wear.

Most houses are built of mud, but the walls of Chitral Fort, laid out amid the chequered green fields on the banks of the Chitral River, are of sturdy stone. Though the stonework is now crumbling, the fort, once the home of the Mehtars, the old rulers of the valley, serves as the police headquarters — set off by the graceful lines of the suspension bridge that spans the river.

In 1895 Surgeon Major Robertson and 400 men were held under siege for forty-eight days by a combined force of the Dir and Chitral rulers. Eventually, Colonel James Kelly led 250 men from Gilgit through the Shandur Pass to relieve the fortress. They covered more than 500 gruelling kilometres in the depth of winter. Thereafter, the British maintained a permanent garrison in Chitral Fort.

It was in Chitral and other reaches of this northern fastness that British cavalry officers and horsemen discovered the sport of polo and exported it to the rest of the world.

Cruder, more vigorous, and certainly far more dangerous than its anglicized version, the sport has been played for centuries. Each year thousands travel to Chitral to enjoy the town's three rugged polo tournaments, held during Chitral's spring festival, and again in June and August.

Tournaments start with competitions aimed at testing each player's prowess with cavalry lance aimed at wooden tent pegs, or cylinders of paper stuck in the ground. The matches are played on an unusually long and narrow field, the thundering hooves raising clouds of dust. The six- or seven-a-side teams heed no rules, run with the same madly galloping ponies throughout, and rouse the partisan crowd to fever-pitch — frequently riding each other off the ground into barricades, or attempting to decapitate each other with wild swings of their mallets. Each time a goal is scored the local band breaks into a cacophony of discordant noise: each player is honoured by his own individual tune, so locals some distance from the event are left in no doubt about the scorer.

Anything goes, including hand-carrying the ball, so long as it crosses the goal line. By comparison, an American Wild West rodeo might pass for choir practice.

Many enthusiasts believe the game derives from the Afghan sport of 'pulling the goat', *buskashi,* which is also played at the Chitral tournaments. Strength, stamina, and courage, as well as superb horsemanship, are needed to participate in this game of games. The aim is for the riders to snatch a dead goat and gallop around the field maintaining possession before dropping it in a circle in the centre of the pitch. The opponents challenge the possessor for the trophy and, with few if any rules, the result is hair-raising enough to make spectators thankful they are merely passive if vociferous witnesses. In time gone by, celebrating the martial heritage of the Afghan Pukhtuns, there was no goat — just a living enemy, or his head.

A century ago, a seven-kilometre-long racecourse was carved out of a piece of flat, stony ground dominated by a mound of earth which the Mehtar used as his regal grandstand. And perched on a 9,000-foot-high plateau above the capital is the now unoccupied summer palace of the Mehtars of Chitral.

Woodcutters stride up to this height easily in about ninety minutes — less than half the time it takes the uninitiated to stumble and slip over the glacial moraine that bars the way.

The palace is a nostalgic evocation of the grand days of the feudal kings, an era when Chitral's fast-declining wildlife, particularly ibex and deer, was abundant. Inside, the trophies still cling to the wall alongside faded sepia photographs of the rulers who shot them.

Set amid green fields and colourful orchards, the palace provides a fine vantage point for the magnificent panorama of the valley against the dramatic centrefold of the Hindu Kush, majestic Tirich Mir. Chitral folklore believes that this 25,290-foot-high peak is guarded by a ring of giant frogs, *boguzai,* and an inner ring of fairies disguised as seductive maidens who meet the climber with bowls of milk or blood. Those who sip the blood, the legend runs, are never seen again.

Their houses perch precariously on the precipitous slopes of their mountainsides — soaring flanks, ravaged by erosion gullies and withered and arid, that climb ever upward, linked by even more precarious footpaths that follow the contours of the slopes above what are virtually sheer drops.

Most Chitralis have a hybrid lineage. They are a mixture of many races and speak Khowar. The majority are Muslims, a quarter of them giving allegiance to the Aga Khan, leader of the world's Ismaili community.

90 For centuries the valley was divided into a series of petty fiefdoms but after

Right: Typical Kalash village in Bumburet Valley.

Right: Kalash mother and child.

Pakistan's Independence, Chitral's administration became the responsibility of the federal Government in 1950. In 1969 the area was absorbed into Pakistan's North-West Frontier Province.

Living echoes of its centuries of isolation still survive in the Kalash valleys of Bumburet, Rambur, and Birir in Chitral's far north where, their history shrouded by mystery and uncertain legend, Pakistan's only pagan community — the 3,000 non-Muslim people of the Kafir Kalash known as the Black Infidels — lives.

Few communities in the world can claim such an inspiring heritage as their mountain valley landscape — a vista of lush green fields studded with fruit orchards, and groves of walnut and plane trees run through by the sparkling ribbons of crystal-clear streams.

Visiting Kafiristan one autumn in the last decade of the nineteenth century, Colonel Durand was overwhelmed by its natural beauty.

*We had gone to visit some more hot springs which came out some hundred feet or so above the road, and the view up the side valley was lovely, a sea of autumn colour in which the gold of the willow shaded off into the dark red of the rose thickets. On our way down we branched off to try and get some shooting. We got none, but were amply rewarded by the magnificent scenery.*

He saw beautiful lakes and rivers and then, riding on horseback to the 16,000-foot crest of the Shui Pass leading into Kafiristan, beheld Tirich Mir.

*The view from the top was grand: right opposite us, with only one range of lower mountains in between, rose Tirich Mir, twenty-five thousand feet high; no cloud obscured the view, and so close did we seem that every turn of the glaciers could be traced, and the lines of the avalanches distinctly seen.*

At that time Kafiristan, the 'country of blacks', extended into Afghan's Nuristan, the 'country of light', providing an ethnical and geographical barrier between the Chitralis and the Afghans. But in 1896 the Nuristan Kalash, the 'Red Kafirs', were forcibly converted to Islam. Not so their kith and kin in Chitral, thus surviving as a twentieth-century anachronism in Islamic Pakistan that has become a powerful magnet, not just for ethnologists and anthropologists, but also for tourists lured by their colourful festivals, cultures, and traditions.

The road to Bumburet twists and winds as it climbs the rumpled, barren mountain slopes to pass over into the valley at 9,000 feet. From this central Kalash Valley you can drive on rough four-wheel drive trails or hike to both Rambur and Birir — though it's a hard slog to Birir over an 8,000-foot-high mountain.

Opposite: Traditional Kalash folk dance.

Opposite: Young Kalash girl picking fruit.

Top: Kalash youngster with cowrie shell headdress.

Above: Kalash youngster with vividly-coloured beaded jewellery.

Dotted around these valleys are about twenty of the picturesque Kalash villages, their compact, rectangular, but windowless two-storey houses made of different layers of timber, stone, and unbaked brick, many set into the side of the cliffs and hills. The cracks in each strata of the building are filled with pebbles. The design has evolved over the centuries to withstand the frequent 'quakes and earth tremors that wrack this meeting place of the continents.

Kalash simply means black — describing the predominant colour of their clothing. Thought by many to be descendants of Alexander the Great's cohorts who stayed and settled in these parts, certainly a number of the Kalash feature fair hair, blue eyes, and are taller than their Chitrali contemporaries.

But the Kalash have no recorded history and their genealogy is lost in the mists of time. Their name resounds, however, in the history of the subcontinent. The Kalash met the hordes of Tamurlane, the earth shaker, in 1398, and those of the Mughal Emperor, Babur, in 1507.

Scotsman William Watts MacNair, the model for Lurgan Sahib in Rudyard Kipling's classic, *Kim,* may well have been the first European to venture into Kalash territory. Kipling also chose Kafiristan — which he never visited — as the setting for his short story, *The Man Who Would Be King,* in which two degenerate Britons become the deities of a primitive and credulous community.

Lost in the limbo of antiquity though they may be, the Kalash are far from primitive. Their traditions and culture deserved, and were given, more serious research and commentary by Surgeon Major Robertson, the hero of the siege of Chitral, who later became the British Political Agent in Gilgit.

Robertson visited the Kalash valleys in 1889 and 1891 and his study, *The Kafirs of the Hindu Kush,* remains a classic: still the best ethnological study of these people who worship a pantheon of strange gods — each a guardian of every eventuality — presided over by Imra, the supreme creator. This ancient religion is a mixture of animism and nature worship, characterized by rituals invoking fire, idol, and ancestor worship.

Two Kalash divinities command special veneration — Mahandeo, the virile warrior guardian god of crops, birds, and hunting, and Jestak, a female goddess who watches over the home and pregnancy, birth, children, love, and marriage.

Passionately fond of music and dance, the Kalash celebrate birth, marriage, and death with three different dances — and mark the changing seasons of the year with a spring festival, harvest festival in mid-summer, a grape and walnut festival in October, and a New Year festival. The dates vary each year but the dancing, singing, drinking, and feasting is a tireless celebration of the

joy of life climaxed with sacrificial goats slaughtered on their smoke-blackened fire altars.

There are some holy places in the Kalash Valley forbidden to their often strikingly beautiful and unveiled women who, over their elaborately braided plaits, wear distinctive black headdresses, decorated with cowrie shells and buttons and crowned with dyed feathers.

Significantly, the Kalash do not bury their dead. They are left in wooden coffins on the ground which soon disintegrate under the onslaught of rain, wind, sun, and snow. Many coffins are ornately carved and the wealthier Kalash also carve wooden effigies to stand beside them. It implies no lack of reverence or love; rather a wish to keep the dead within the community.

Wherever you go in Chitral, beauty and adventure await the wanderer. Here the hardy and experienced begin their treks through the high passes of the Hindu Kush that form one side of the narrow Afghan panhandle that divides the Soviet Union from Pakistan. Along the Rich Valley you trail over vertiginous tracks that often appear to plunge — terrifyingly — straight down the vertical cliff face until you come to the 13,980-foot-high Shah Jinali Pass. The ascent to the spectacular summit is usually deep in snow.

You can then follow the trails along and beneath the ridgebacks of these daunting mountains to 15,000-foot-high Darkot Pass, the way of the Chinese invaders more than a thousand years ago, down into Gilgit and the riven tangled heart of the spectacular ravines and peaks.

# 4 The Roof of the World

Pierced by the deepest ravines and gorges on earth, so narrow that even in summer the sun is visible for only three hours a day, blasted and pummelled by icy winds that never cease to blow, the highest land in the world rejoices in the name of 'Little Tibet'.

No diminutive this, though. Baltistan's 26,000 square kilometres, crowned by the majesty of K-2, at 28,250 feet the world's second-highest mountain, sit at an average height of more than 15,000 feet. On a contour map the defiles between them form a skein of microthin lines, like the veins and creases that wrinkle the seamed and weary faces of the ancients that live in the perpetual shadows of these rock monoliths.

Little Tibet's larger neighbour, the Gilgit Agency, is scarcely less higher nor much less scarred by precipitous ravine and gully.

No relief map or guide book can lead you through this wilderness of lost horizons. There are none. The horizons merge in a tumultuous maze in which west and east, north and south, lurch giddily from one side of the eye to the other in utter confusion.

Flying towards them from the south, in the jet stream at 30,000 feet, a ridge of cotton wool clouds, shadowed by a mass of brooding, anvil-shaped *cumulonimbus,* begins to draw near.

Jagged peaks, some black and fearsome, others ice-white, lurk within the sea of cloud. Occasionally, there's a break in the fortress-like ramparts — one of the few passes through the almost impenetrable Roof of the World. Elsewhere, the clouds billow, like white caps on the ocean, and break on the rocky shores of these reefs in the sky.

As mountains go, the Karakoram are young. The peak of K-2 is made of marine rock of the Cretaceous age which formed the bed of the Tethys Sea when it ebbed and flowed here between eighty and sixty million years ago. Then, at the end of the Mesozoic era, grinding and crunching, the continents met, forcing up the bed of the Tethys Sea, foot by foot, until it tipped the sky.

At wing-tip level, west to east, the panorama — embracing also the Hindu Kush, Pamirs, the Himalaya, and the lesser ranges — stretches as far as the eye can see. And the few large areas of table land that do exist in such a perpendicular wilderness stretch out their strangely horizontal plateaux at heights above 15,000 feet.

Looking down it seems impossible that anyone, or anything, could live within the frozen embrace of these peaks. Yet, locked in a dozen secret valleys, reached only by fragile footpaths sometimes carved out of the side of a sheer rock face hundreds of feet above a rocky river gorge, lie tiny, forgotten kingdoms.

Bleak granite cliffs, almost sheer, rise from one to six kilometres high on

Opposite: Powder puff cloud caresses the shoulders of 24,299-feet-high Haramosh in Baltistan.

Previous pages: Some of the world's greatest glaciers, interlinked like a giant road system, all merge in the great natural amphitheatre of Concordia overshadowed, within a radius of twenty-five kilometres, by ten of the world's thirty greatest mountains. The mountain at left is Chogolisa, 25,027, and second from right, Marble Peak, 20,469 feet. The glacier in the immediate foreground is the Godwin-Austen. At the extreme right in the foreground is the K2 base camp. From left to right the other glaciers are: Upper Baltoro and Vigne, meeting in Concordia, and (extreme right) the Savoia Glacier.

every side. These jagged barren spurs, devoid of any vegetation, are broken beneath by expanses of rocky alpine desert. And from the great glaciers above, vast reserves of water filter slowly away during summer to nourish the Indus watershed.

The Siachen, Baltoro, and other glaciers of the Karakoram are the largest and longest in the world outside the polar region. From its spectacular birthplace in Concordia, at the base of K-2 and the Gasherbrum range, the Baltoro Glacier flows for more than fifty-nine kilometres, while the Batura Glacier to the north, hanging over the Karakoram Highway, streams down from the northernmost ramparts of the Hindu Kush, flowing for almost sixty-five kilometres, and the Siachen Glacier, off K-2, runs for more than seventy kilometres.

These glaciers are essential to the existence of Pakistan's 100 million people, most of whom live in the dry, subtropical plains of the Indus basin. For only in these great glaciers above 9,000 feet is there any yearly surplus of moisture.

Yet, ironically, the more it rains and snows, the less water is released. Cloud cover restricts the summer melt. Other dynamic characteristics of this clash between the continents affect the people of Pakistan and their major water resource. The steep slopes, extreme heights, sudden weather changes, and frequent earthquakes, often cause chaos on a gargantuan scale.

Dramatic avalanches, landslides, mudflows, and moving glaciers create a cataclysmic landscape threatening villages and roadblocks. Devastating floods occur when a newly-formed glacial lake broaches its natural dam and leaps forward to inundate everything in its path.

Yet, despite this unpredictable environment, the mountains with the highest mean elevation on earth serve as sanctuary for the last substantial populations of Himalayan wildlife — ibex, markhor, mountain sheep like the Marco Polo and Ovis Ammon, musk deer, wolf, and snow leopard.

But the new roads carved to once-isolated communities like Askole, the highest village in the region — perhaps in the world — in the gorge of the Braldo River just below the Biafo Glacier which feeds it, now bring tourists, poachers, and hunters, and this Himalayan faunal reservoir is under threat.

Policing illicit hunting and local poaching is virtually impossible. In the magazine *International Wildlife,* Galen Rowell, author of *In the Throne Room of the Mountain Gods,* recalls trekking in the region a few years ago when his guide counted the spoor of more than 100 ibex on the fresh snow cover of a glacier —together with the spoor of their pursuers, three hunters and two dogs.

*In the weeks to come we saw more than 300 ibex and evidence of three other sets of poachers.*

Opposite: Smiling youngsters in the secret valley of Misghar.

Overleaf: Suspension bridge over the Hunza River near Gilgit.

Left: Three Gilgit postboxes —
colour-coded for mail for
different regions.

In Askole he was offered the skin of a snow leopard for US$500. 'One of the region's estimated twenty-five remaining snow leopard had been killed by a lone shepherd with a wooden club while it slept. He had tracked the rare cat to its lair after it killed one of his goats, knowing that on the black market a single skin could bring him a year's earnings.'

The greater menace, however, is not local poaching, but rich hunters who use their wealth and influence to stalk through the *nullahs* of The Roof of the World cutting down fast-diminishing species.

The lore of the wild is writ long in the legends and cultures of the locals. Hundreds of years ago they carved pictures of the animals that then roamed these ravaged mountains in their thousands. The most common rock and cave images depict ibex.

Before a hunt, no man would sleep with his wife because he believed that if he did so a pagan fairy would fail to appear in his dreams to tell him where his prey could be found.

Rowell conveys his sense of sadness, too, that the new links are destroying something equally precious — the changeless pattern of human society that has existed so long.

*I have seen a number of cultures once thought to be timeless and immutable change before my eyes. . . . Who would deny the people of Askole access to what we take for granted in the rest of the world? . . . Yet something equally vital will be lost in the process. Ties to the past. Ties to our own past; to a time when the human race lived closer to the land with little effect on its wildness. . . . the true Shangri-la [is] not a certain a place that can be visited, but a state of mind that has already passed in much of the Himalaya.*

This change is very recent. The first European known to have seen the Karakoram Mountains in perspective — Godfrey Thomas Vigne — standing on the edge of the 17,000-foot heights of the frozen Deosai Plains, on 6 September 1835, was overwhelmed by the vision. 'Wherever the eye could rove, arose, with surpassing grandeur, a vast assemblage of the enormous summits that compose the Tibetan Himalaya.'

In his 1977 book, *When Men & Mountains Meet*, John Keay wrote: 'The discovery of this massive mountain system flanking the northern banks of the Shyok and Indus from Leh to Hunza put a whole new complexion on the western Himalayas.'

Winter is long and summer brief in The Roof of the World among the gable cliffs, ice cornices, vaulted pillars, sliding glaciers, and rock buttresses chipped and carved by the cutting edge of the sub-zero blasts into strange and eerie sculptures. Frequently lashed by 150-kilometre-an-hour blizzards

Opposite: Fruit bazaar in Gilgit
with lush fruits grown in
remote and hidden valleys.

Opposite right: Hot food
vendor in Gilgit bazaar.

Opposite: Selection of typical
Chitral and Hunza hats.

Opposite right: Roadside
puncture repair in Gilgit's busy
main street.

that threaten to hurl everything, even whole mountains, into the abysses below, winds in the Karakoram are among the most powerful in the world. Only in late May or early June do the snowclad passes open, some to close again in September. Constantly on the move, pitted with deadly unseen crevasses thousands of feet deep, the glaciers add the finishing touch to the most dramatic, if desolate, landscape in the world.

Vigne brought back the first accounts of this, one of the world's greatest glacial systems, at a time when geographers were sceptical — as they were about ice on the Equator — that any glaciers could exist in a warmer latitude than that of the European Alps.

He was stunned by their enormity. Passing the tail of the Chogo Lungma Glacier which streams down the south-eastern slopes of the Rakaposhi Range, he measured it as close to a kilometre wide and thirty metres thick. From a cavern beneath its clear green ice flowed a river shunting massive blocks of ice with a noise like cannon. Colonel H. H. Godwin-Austen, after whom one of the glaciers is named, added graphic insight into the system through his sketches and observations.

'What no drawing can capture,' writes John Keay, however, 'but which his narrative emphasizes so well is the instability of it all. In the early hours of the morning when the frost grips everything it seems like a silent, timeless unchangeable world. But in summer by mid-afternoon all hell may break loose.'

One afternoon Godwin-Austen was roused from an after lunch siesta by 'an unusual, rumbling sound' and shouting. He scrambled to his feet. Bearing down from the boulder bed of a side valley shot a ten-metre-wide, two-metre-deep wall of mud and rocks 'like peas shot out of a bag'. Summer sun had freed a stream frozen for months by an advancing glacier.

As some glaciers retreat, leaving in their ebb a bed of treacherous moraine, a detritus of mud and rock split by frost from mountain walls, others advance, overwhelming lakes and valleys, campsites, and streams. 'Some appear sleek and white on the flank of a mountain,' writes Keay, 'but visit their vicinity, try to ascend them and you find them surrounded by an oozing morass of mud and stone, blocks of ice and shattered rock, as insecure and unpleasant to cross as the worst ice field. This is the world as it must have been at the dawn of creation, cracking and crumbling, oozing and flowing with irresistible elemental forces. No place at all for human beings.'

This constant movement creates one of the most distinct phenomena of life in the Karakoram — the endless, anguished creaking of rock and ice in mortal combat, moaning as if in agony and sometimes drowned in the tearing, screaming, thundering frenzy of an avalanche.

Above: Chinar Bagh monument in Gilgit commemorates those who died in the 1947-48 struggle against Gilgit's Dogra ruler, a Hindu.

Some idea of the perils of crossing these deceptively stable-looking coverings of ice and snow, only to plunge into the bottomless abyss of a crevasse beneath, can be gathered from the accounts of Victorian travellers and explorers.

Godwin-Austen, who 'found them ugly things to look into, much more so to cross', tried to test the depth of one that went down 'into darkness between walls garnished with magnificent green icicles from six to twenty feet long and of proportionate thickness'. But all his ropes tied together measured only 162 feet, 'which was not enough'.

*The Times* of London correspondent, E. F. Knight, in his turn of the century adventure, *Where Three Empires Meet*, told of his experience on Nanga Parbat:

*Higher up I crossed a slope of boulders and debris on which roses and other bushes were growing. I naturally concluded that I was walking on the solid surface, when, to my surprise, I suddenly came upon a great chasm, and looking into it, saw dark caverns opening out under me, with walls of solid ice: while in places the ice had melted away, leaving the crust of moraine above unsupported. The water was fast dripping down from the roofs of these icy caverns, and rocks were continually tumbling in from above as the thaw proceeded.*

He came across many more of these melting glaciers, fascinated by the sight of uprooted rose-trees, still in bloom, lying among blocks of ice and fallen boulders far down at the bottom of some dim chasm.

Botanist Dr Thomas Thomson, the first scientist to explore the Karakoram watershed, which is almost entirely glacier-fed unlike the eastern Himalaya, remembered he found it difficult to describe the extreme desolation:

*I had nowhere before seen a country so utterly waste . . . a rocky precipice, worn and furrowed in every direction and broken into sharp pinnacles, rose to the height of at least two thousand feet, overhanging a steep ravine, while to right and left mountain was heaped upon mountain in inextricable confusion, large patches of snow covering the higher parts.*

The extremes of temperature experienced in this wilderness are the most severe in the world. In summer rocks become so hot that they blister the skin. In the long winter it is the coldest place where man lives permanently. A veteran of the Arctic and Alaska, Lord Dunmore, who crossed The Roof of the World in 1892, recording 40° of frost inside his tent, pronounced it the coldest place on earth.

Combined with constant living at altitudes of 12,000 feet or more, the cutting edge of the winds that blast against mountain peak and funnel

Opposite: Polo match at Gilgit where the game was born.

Above: Youngster learns the first essentials of the sport of kings on Gilgit's polo field.

Opposite: Thundering hooves and swirling dust during rugged polo match in Gilgit town.

Overleaf left: Early morning sun bathes the 23,840-feet-high summit of Diran above the Minapin Glacier.

Overleaf right: Silvered magic — 25,552-feet-high Rakaposhi, known in the language of the Hunza people as Dumani, 'the mother of mist', gleams above the fabled kingdom of Hunza, the valley that inspired James Hilton's 'Lost Horizon'.

furiously over high pass and along ravine give fresh scale to concepts of endurance and hardihood. 'Capricious in direction,' writes Keay, 'unpredictable in strength and unimpeded by anything approaching shelter, it blew day and night, summer and winter, on the mountains and in the valleys, with a vicious numbing intent.'

Such a tangled knot of mighty peaks also gives new scale to human perspectives. There are no comparisons. The clasp of mountains that decorates the world's midriff is unique. From 'the veritable top of the world', the 18,000-foot-high Depsang Plains on the Tibetan Plateau in the east, Indian Army Surgeon Major H. W. Bellew described his impressions:

*All around appeared mountain ranges, none of which were less than 20,000 feet high, while to the west rose two peaks of much greater height; yet in the distance they seemed below us, for the land around sloped away down on all sides. In whichever direction we looked the sky appeared below us and the world slunk out of sight. In fact, we felt as if we had risen above the world . . .*

Roughly 500,000 people inhabit the 70,000 square kilometres of Pakistan's northern areas, which consist of the old Gilgit and Baltistan agencies and the former fiefdoms of Hunza and Nagar, now divided into three administrative districts.

For centuries almost the entire area remained unexplored — not due so much to lack of interest as to the fact that there was no access. Articles of common daily use, which had to be hauled long distances by pack beasts along perilous footpaths, were either unavailable or cost so much most people could not afford them.

A 'Silk Route' through these desolate mountain fastnesses had long existed. Regardless of the hazards, traders and mule trains had carried silk, tea, and porcelain from China over this tortuous route, via the Khunjerab and Karakoram passes, to the subcontinent to barter for gold, ivory, jewels, and spices for more than 2,000 years. The traders rode through tiny valleys where feudal kingdoms held sway: Pasu, Hunza, Chalt, Nomal, and Gilgit, but virtually none ventured off the trail to the other tiny fiefdoms, like Yasin, Dunial, and Skardu, unknown to all but their own and the neighbouring communities.

After Gilgit, at Besham in Kohistan, the Silk Route cut west over the Shangla Pass to Swat. But apart from these trade caravans, Gilgit, the capital of the area, and the other princedoms, were long cut off from the outside world. Until 1891 the only fair weather footpath to Gilgit from Kashmir in the south was over the hazardous 13,700-foot-high Burzil pass, through the Astore Valley, to Bunji: the journey took about a month. In 1892, another

route was opened through the Kaghan Valley and across the 13,685-foot-high Babusar Pass. Both were only open for three months of the year before the snows fell again.

Thus, hidden within their girdles of ice-encrusted peaks, these valley states maintained a changeless way of life. They were opened up by the Karakoram Highway, which in the course of its 883-kilometre-long journey from Thakot rises, through the Himalaya and the Karakoram Mountains, to more than 16,000 feet and is one of the great engineering marvels of the world.

Started officially under a 1966 Sino-Pak agreement, it took twelve long, perilous years to complete as it carved its way through the greatest mountain ranges in the world.

Linking Islamabad to China, in the north the highway cuts through the picturesque valleys of Hunza and Nagar, to the Chinese border which lies across the frozen wastes of 16,200-foot-high Khunjerab Pass.

The seven-metre-wide road involved thirty million cubic yards of earth works and rock cuts and consumed 800 tons of explosives, 80,000 tons of cement, 35,000 tons of coal, and 80,000 tons of fuel and lubricants as a thousand trucks maintained a constant shuttle shipping supplies, men, and equipment up and down its length.

For almost every kilometre prised loose from the unrelenting grip of this mountain domain, a man died.

Eighty-five bridges and many tunnels mark the course of the highway. At Gilgit, the Chinese-built bridge is distinguished by the lions carved on its structure, representing the Chinese god who keeps all safe in a storm.

Above the bridge stands the tranquil cemetery, shaded by trees, where the Chinese workers killed while building the highway — those the lion failed — lie in eternal peace. It's surrounded by the mountains, including 25,550-foot-high Rakaposhi, that they fought and conquered but which claimed their revenge.

Twelve years of blasting shook whole mountains. One perennial problem is the movement of the Pasu and Batura Glaciers beyond Hunza. But since it opened the highway has never been closed for longer than a day at a time except once, when Batura Glacier crashed down on it and the debris took three days to clear.

And, even today, though now linked to the mainstream of national life through the Karakoram and Skardu Highways, the isolated communities they serve remain much of an anachronism — their cultures and customs a living evocation of medieval feudalism.

The southern extremities of the Pamir Knot are marked by the Gurais and Burzil passes from Srinagar in Indian-occupied Kashmir. Set 13,000 feet

Opposite: Rare ibex on the winter slopes of Naltar Valley beneath the high Shani Pass.

Overleaf: Sunlight gleams on the peak that dominates the horizon at the head of the Naltar Valley where the Shani Pass crosses over into the heart of the Pamir Knot at a height of 15,750 feet.

Opposite: Emerald-green, terraced fields of Chalt form verdant counterpoint to the barren and arid mountains where the Karakoram Highway follows the course of the Hunza River.

Right: Happy bridegroom dances for joy on the Karakoram Highway in anticipation of his impending marriage.

above sea level, covered with deep snow and ice for more than half the year, the desolate Deosai Plains, atop the pass, stretch for more than nineteen kilometres. Weather changes are sudden. Storms blow up in seconds and the deceptive calm of a blue sky suddenly becomes a screaming maelstrom of roaring winter blizzards or icy summer winds and rain or hail.

Many have been trapped and frozen to death, but on a clear day there's a dramatic view of the Pamir Knot's major southern buttress — Nanga Parbat, sixth-highest mountain in the world, It's the westernmost anchor of the great Himalaya range that curves like a scimitar more than 2,500 kilometres across the subcontinent from Nanga Parbat in the west to Burma in the east.

Vigne describes his sense of awe when he reached the top of the pass and arrived on the Deosai Plains:

*. . . the stupendous peak of Diarmul [Heavenly mount] or Nanga Parbat, more than forty miles [sixty-four kilometres] distant in a straight line, but appearing to be much nearer, burst upon my sight, rising far above every other around it and entirely cased in snow excepting where its scarps were too precipitous for it to remain upon them. It was partially encircled by a broad belt of cloud and its finely pointed summit glistening in the full blaze of the morning sun, relieved by the clear blue sky beyond it, presented on account of its isolated situation an appearance of extreme altitude . . .*

He was looking at its southern flanks, which form one of the world's greatest precipices — a sheer drop of almost seven kilometres.

In the west, seen from the Karakoram Highway, the panorama is just as awesome, even though the ramparts here slope rather than plunge down. Wherever the Indus Valley broadens out it dominates the horizon.

For sheer size Nanga Parbat is almost without equal — not a single peak but, in fact, an entire massif culminating in an ice summit 26,660 feet high. The rumpled flanks of its subservient attendants climb up out of the Indus Valley and there, beyond the blue-grey whaleback ridges, ringed by a halo cloud, rises its long ridge. Of all the great mountains that form The Roof of the World it is the most frequently seen.

Unequalled for scale, so is it for hostility. Apart from Everest and Annapurna in the south, it has claimed the lives of more climbers than any other — close to fifty at the last count. It was first conquered in 1953 by an Austro-German expedition. The world's greatest mountaineer, Reinhold Messner, made the first solo ascent in 1979.

In the world league of the fourteen peaks higher than 8,000 metres — 26,250 feet — K-2 and Nanga Parbat are considered the two most difficult. The climate all around the mountain — in the Astore Valley and others — reflects

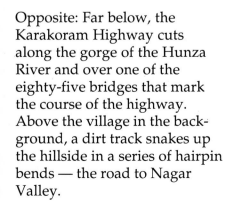

Opposite: Far below, the Karakoram Highway cuts along the gorge of the Hunza River and over one of the eighty-five bridges that mark the course of the highway. Above the village in the background, a dirt track snakes up the hillside in a series of hairpin bends — the road to Nagar Valley.

its own natural savagery.

Trekkers who brave the Babusar Pass out of the Kaghan Valley descend to Chilas, which marks the gateway into the Gilgit Agency, at the southern base of Nanga Parbat. It's the old Silk Route, and the rocks and cliffs around Chilas testify to the centuries of perilous trade that passed this way. Here the Indus Valley broadens for 130 kilometres. It became the traditional crossing place of the Indus and through the centuries a crossroads of trade, pilgrimage, and history. Pilgrims, travellers, and trade caravans all paused to rest here after their lung-sapping labours in either direction, drawing breath for the next challenge that lay ahead.

While they rested in the chaotic, boulder-strewn landscape that surrounds this fifth-century 'City of the Moon', *Somanagara*, they inscribed the scattered rocks and standing cliffs with images and hieroglyphics that gave thanks for a safe journey, served to ward off evil, and comforted those who would follow in their perilous footsteps. These stylized images of animals like the ibex and horses, festivals and riotous drinking parties, slave caravans and worshippers, royal couples and ploughmen, Buddhist stupas and religious symbols, form one of the great treasuries of upper Indus art. These carvings, and images and primitive tools from an earlier era, cover an epoch that continued for more than 5,000 years.

The land is bleak and arid, the soil leached by the fierce summer sun and the dry, cold winter, eroded by the constant gales that funnel down into this bowl, replenished by great deposits of flood silt from the Indus. 'The scenery around [the plains of Bunji] is woefully barren,' wrote Knight, 'the Indus flowing through an undulating waste of stones while the enclosing mountains were destitute of vegetation.'

Yet, remarkably, all the way from Dassu, the mid-way stage between Patan and Chilas on the Karakoram Highway to Chilas, every ten or twenty kilometres great stands of hewn, four-square timber crowd the roadside — plucked from the lush, high-altitude forests of the invisible peaks above and hefted down the precipitous slopes with excruciating labour.

So desolate is the land, so hostile were the people, that the British avoided the area like the plague until the 1890s when, improbably, they began to fancy that the Silk Route might make the road for an invasion from Russia or China. Wrote Knight:

*The maps indicate the course of the river from near this point to where it emerges into British territory by dotted lines, to signify that it has never been surveyed; while the word ''unexplored'', so tempting to the traveller's imagination, is written large across the region. From here one looks down the*

Opposite: Rugged 24,000-feet-high eastern face of Bojoahaghur Dunasir rises above the ancient 900-year-old Mir of Hunza's palace at Baltit.

Overleaf: Karimabad sprawls down the mountainside beneath Baltit Fort while in the background the stunning grandeur of Rakaposhi dominates Hunza Valley.

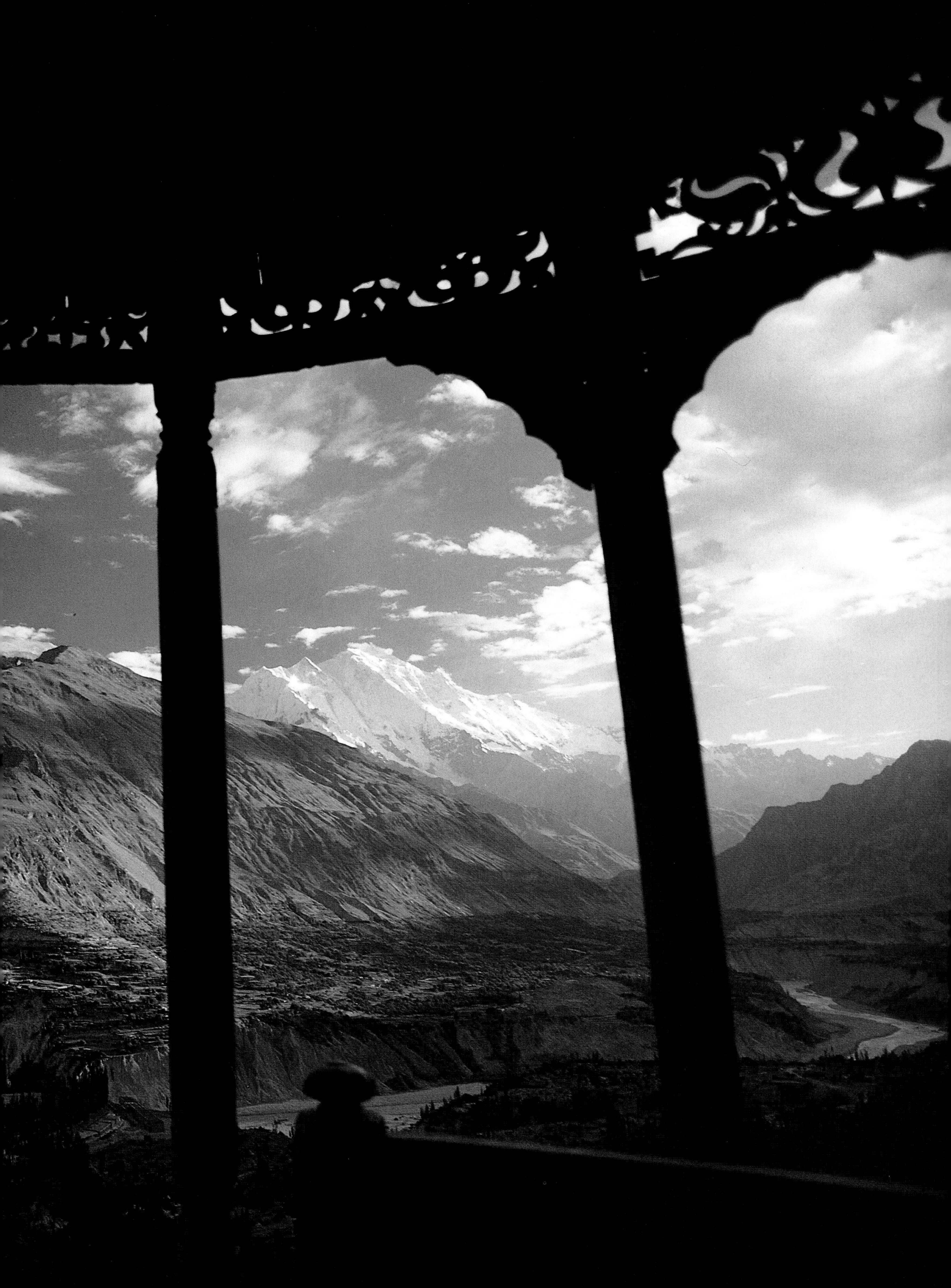

Left: Modern new palace of the Mir of Hunza at Karimabad.

Left: Rock carvings at Ganesh, alongside the Karakoram Highway, beneath Altit fort in the Hunza Valley, are between 1,500 and 3,000 years old.

*valley into the mysterious and forbidden land that is so near, and from the
upper Hattu Pir road, by which I returned, the first Chilas village, Gor, with
its surrounding orchards, is visible.*

So, although virtually the whole of this part of the upper Indus was then
unknown, the British began to develop a foot road from Srinagar to Gilgit
where they had already established a presence. They planned another over
the Babusar Pass to protect their flank and supply routes from the fanatical
tribesmen of Chilas.

It was north of Chilas, on the vale of Bunji, near Knight's observation post
on the Hattu Pir, in 1840, that a tremendous convulsion shook The Roof of the
World and 'a whole mountain suddenly fell into the Indus', creating a dam
that was broached the next year by another tremor, causing the catastrophic
flood that swept over the Peshawar Plains.

The name Bunji signifies the figure fifty in local vernacular and was
bestowed on the vale because fifty villages were overwhelmed by the deep
eighty-kilometre-long lake that swiftly backed up behind the natural dam
within the space of six months. Now all is desert.

In summer Knight found it 'an infernal oven, like a stokehole'. All along the
Indus between Chilas and Bunji the valley is a moonscape of arid remnant
glaciers and jagged peaks above which, wherever you turn, broods the great
mountain juggernaut. In her book, *The Lion River*, Jean Fairley quotes one
mountaineer, W. M. Conway:

*I had never seen any valley that compared to it either in kind or in
dimensions. It was as barren as an Arabian wady; it was floored with the
strewn ruins of countless floods, bleached and blasted by the suns of countless
summers; it was walled along by rocky cliffs, a maze of precipices and gullies.
. . . The naked skeleton of the world stood forth, with every stratum displayed
and every mark of the sculpturing chisel undisguised.*

Lined by mountains on either side, rising from 7,000 to 26,000 feet, in some
sections this valley is no wider than two-and-a-half kilometres. Yet in the
early days of independence, where no plane had ever flown, Dakotas of the
Pakistan Air Force with a ceiling of 10,000 feet flew daily supply sorties along
it for many months. With no room to manoeuvre, pilots called it the 'Valley of
No Return'. Weather was unpredictable and the valleys by any aviation
standards unnavigable.

Pilots of Pakistan International Airlines pioneered the civil route in Fokker
Friendships many years ago. The daily services from Islamabad International
Airport to Gilgit and Skardu must be the most dramatic scheduled flights in

commercial aviation. Passengers flying beneath the Nanga Parbat massif feel as if they can reach out and touch the mountain wall on either side. 'It's just like flying down a roofless tunnel,' said one exhilarated passenger after landing at Gilgit, where a sheer rock wall looms up beyond the end of the runway.

PIA has a morning schedule but it is weather, not time, that rules airline punctuality in this region.

The raging winds that once broke up a C-130 Hercules freighter in the 1960s are just as daunting a hazard as the mountains themselves. When weather closes in, safety-conscious PIA close down the flights. In summer, this sometimes means a large backlog of passengers builds up at either end.

No matter the excitement of the flight, the minute you leave the airfield you walk into a time-warp. Though now the most bustling bazaar on the Silk Route, dusty Gilgit still seems to hang suspended in the limbo of a forgotten long ago.

Once the most isolated outpost of any in the British Empire — at a time when the Empire was at its zenith — there's an immediate sense of distance, of isolation, of time removed from the twentieth century, despite the obvious presence of a large army, and the continual stream of traffic on the other side of the river where the Karakoram Highway clings to the eastern wall of the narrow valley.

No longer the Indus, here the crystal-bright waters that bounce over the rocks, sparkling in the spring sunlight, are the Gilgit and the Hunza rivers. Just a few kilometres downstream from Gilgit, almost at the point where the north-flowing giant turns its back on the impenetrable mountains which hold it fast and heads south by south-west, they join the Indus.

By Karakoram standards, Gilgit Valley is broad — dominated by perhaps the loveliest of all northern Pakistan's mountains. Rakaposhi's elegant, 25,550-foot-high spire hangs suspended above the terraced fields of grain and rice and the flowering apricot orchards, and those that look long enough — and there are few that don't — sometimes get the feeling that it could fall inward on to the valley floor.

Colourful cloths and beautiful Chinese silk fluttering in the breeze, fruit, spices, and the staple of the region — dried apricots — give the sprawling bazaar that stretches kilometres down the main street a vivid Technicolor aspect. In these improbable emporiums, Chinese goods — ceramics, cutlery, electronic products — range alongside beautifully crafted local handicrafts, shawls, woollens, baskets, batiks, even old-fashioned ski-boots.

Muezzins call the faithful to prayer from the minarets of the many mosques. A melting pot of a town, more than a third of Gilgit's cosmopolitan mix of

130

Opposite: Princess Bulbul's tower, a slender finger of rock that rises sheer for 2,000 feet above Karimabad, beneath the 24,000-feet summit of Bojoahaghur Dunasir in Hunza Valley.

Overleaf: Cloud frets around the dome of 23,840-feet-high Diran as seen from Karimabad in the Hunza Valley.

Opposite: Crumbling plaster work and missing windows fail to defile the sturdy grace of 900-year-old Baltit Fort.

Left: 200-year-old private mosque of an Ismaili family in Gulmit.

Left: Schoolgirls study their Islamic heritage at Gulmit.

Left: Traditional string music instrument of the Hunza Valley.

Kashgaris, Tshins, Chitralis, Pukthuns, and Hunzakuts, belong to the Aga Khan's Ismaili sect. The greetings carved on the tall cliffs on the east wall of the valley, to catch his eye when he flew in on a ceremonious visit in the early 1980s, still proclaim Gilgit's joy at playing host to the leader of the world's Ismailis. At least 350 different vernaculars and local dialects ring through the constant hubbub of the bazaar.

Maharajahs or Mirs no longer rule over this once-upon-a-time kingdom which, though long a strategic centre that dominated 2,000 years of trade along the Silk Route, has little recorded history. Pagans were fire worshippers before the advent of Buddhism, then Hindu before the advent of Islam. It was invaded and subjugated around AD 750 by a Chinese force of 10,000.

These also occupied Baltistan before being ejected in turn by the Tibetans. Their reign, too, was brief — commemorated by five lines of ancient script, recording the history of the Tibetan rulers. They were carved on a rock outside the town where one of the town's treasures, a seventh-century Buddhist tract was found when three ancient stupas were excavated in 1934.

But by the nineteenth century, when the Silk Route had fallen into disuse, the Muslim valley came under the suzerainty of the Hindu Maharajahs of Kashmir. Briefly in 1877 the British established a power base in the town, but with too small an attachment for defence it was overwhelmed four years later.

Then in 1889, in the name of Queen Victoria, Colonel Algernon Durand was posted to take command of the area, the most isolated outpost of the British Empire, forming a paramilitary police force, the Gilgit Scouts. Wearing the Black Watch tartan and marched into battle by pipers, the Scouts continue still — proud possessors of a famous martial legacy that combines the valour of the hill soldiers of the subcontinent with that of the Highlanders of Scotland.

Defiantly, in 1948 when Gilgit broke with Kashmir and joined Muslim Pakistan, the Scouts Pipe Band marched out into the open of the town's polo field as the Indian Air Force's vintage World War II bombers lumbered in to blitz the town, piping their contempt in the form of such lilting and stirring marches as 'Scotland the Brave'. The rest of the unit was in the front line in Baltistan.

It's on the polo ground that some of the most exciting polo tournaments in the world are fought out with heated, passionate, and ever brave enthusiasm. The major event is staged in November to mark Independence Day. Nearby a stone memorial honours the many brave men who died in the early struggle against Kashmir.

Broad and fertile, just 4,000 feet above sea level, Gilgit is glorious in spring

Above: Young Hunzakut schoolgirl in colourful dress.

Above: Father and daughter fetching water in the Himalayan foothills.

Overleaf left: Dramatic glacier cuts a deep gorge through the Masherbrum range to enter Saltoro Glacier in Baltistan's Hushe Valley in north-east Pakistan.

Overleaf right: Arched symmetrical pillars of rock form the Passu 'Cathedral' in Gulmit Valley.

when the apple, pear, almond, apricot, mulberry, and walnut orchards blossom. Tall plane trees, upright as guardsmen, poplars, eucalyptus, and leafy willows stand sentinel around the well-tended terraces. The little lanes and trails make easy and ideal walking and the mountain foothills are gentle at first.

Near Gilgit one of the longest suspension bridges in Asia — a trembling, graceful 650-foot-wide structure of wood and steel cable anchored only by its support towers in the cliffs — crosses the Hunza river. It leads on to another suspension bridge that crosses the Gilgit river into the town centre. Crossing it — in equally perpetual motion — is the constant stream of life of far northern Pakistan: an old man from Sinkiang, China, watches shish kebabs sizzle over his charcoal fire, Chinese dumplings steam in old saucepans, and everywhere there are the blue-eyed Hunzakuts.

Just a few kilometres west of the town is a stunning three-metre-high image of Buddha carved on a rock cliff 160 feet above the ground. It's near the stupas where the Gilgit manuscripts were uncovered in the 1930s.

Lakes and rivers in the valley teem with plump trout — the Gilgit hatchery is based near one of the valley's small hydroelectric projects on the floor of a narrow and precipitous ravine just a few miles north of the town. Introduced to the region by the British, the trout flourish in the fast-flowing, glacier-fed crystal clear streams which provide them with a perfect environment.

Walking here in the shadows of the greatest peaks on earth is an experience that lingers a lifetime. Once you step off the Karakoram Highway you step back in time — perhaps hundreds of years — to wander over daunting passes that suddenly open out on another hidden jewel, valleys of incomparable beauty, scree walls plunging down to dazzling green meadowlands studded with colourful wild flowers and fertile fields.

Encircled by its cluster of ice peaks, its fields shaded by stands of chinar trees and willows of deepest green, Yasin remains a feudal kingdom still untouched but now, after centuries of strife, at peace. It's one of the most remote of the valleys in the Gilgit area, lying at the foot of the Hindu Kush range, slightly north of the road from Punial, another ancient kingdom of 17,000 subjects which only ended its autonomy as recently as 1972.

The capital, Sher Qila — 'Lion's Fort' — earned its name because it was unconquerable. Its citizens know it best, though, as the place where heaven and earth meet.

This western region of Gilgit offers unbridled adventure. The 225-kilometre-long trail through Punial, Gakuch, and Gupis to Yasin in the north and the Shandur Pass in the west is rough going at its best. Unpredictable, too, because no one knows in advance whether the bridges built the year before

Previous pages: Light and shadow in the daunting ravine followed by the Karakoram Highway close to its highest point, the Khunjerab Pass, where the road joins with one from China.

Left: Traditional Gulmit homestead with grandmother, daughter-in-law, and children.

Left: Drying apricots in the summer sun at Gulmit with Passu 'Cathedral' in far background.

Above: Reaping the harvest at Misghar.

still stand after the season of avalanches and mudslides. But many toil on — at least as far as the azure waters of trout-filled Phandar Lake.

North-east from Gilgit, the gorge of the Hunza River, spawned in the glacier melt beneath the 20,786-foot-high peak of the Ghujerab mountains and enriched by the cascades from the Batura Glacier, is one of the most dramatic on earth. It is eerie and weird. Howling winds scream like banshees, hurling themselves against the towering granite walls.

The early travellers along the Silk Route were brave and determined men. In places the gorge narrows so dramatically that, even at midday, virtually all light vanishes. Great boulders as big as office blocks, thrown down from above during the frequent earth tremors, litter the river bed. When it's not in spate, sulphur yellows the dry river bed and, among the gravel and iron pyrites, garnets lie waiting to be scooped up. Nothing lives here except the cold and the wind. Some of the ravines close in for long distances, as much as eight kilometres of sheer rock face climbing staggeringly high into the sky.

The gem-like tarns and glacier streams of 10,000-foot-high Naltar Valley, in the shadow of graceful Rakaposhi, offer not only hardy anglers joy, but trekkers and ski enthusiasts, too. Dotted with sparse stands of pine, the Pakistan Armed Forces installed two lifts on the valley's steep-sided walls to make it one of the few ski resorts in northern Pakistan.

Trekkers walk on up the valley to Naltar Lake and Shani to cross over the 15,750-foot-high Dianter Pass into perhaps Gilgit's loveliest alpine valley. There's also a trekking trail over 13,836-foot-high Naltar Pass that follows a rugged route to Pakhor.

Just a few kilometres out of Gilgit there's another memorial to the Army men who died building the KKH and 'chose to make the Karakoram there permanent abode'. The tribute reads,

'There shall be:- In their rich dust, a richer dust concealed.'

Nomal is the first sizable settlement after Gilgit and then, on a handsome plateau, at a bend on the river where two gorges from the outliers of the Hindu Kush meet the Hunza river, stands Chalt and its old fortress. It was the farthest outpost of the Maharajah of Kashmir's little empire, ultimately of the British who provided his regime with defence.

Knight found that within its square walls and towers there was room for hundreds of men. But what captured his imagination more was the setting:

*I ascended the heights above Chalt, in order to obtain a view of that magnificent mountain, Rakaposhi, which was well seen from here. Unlike Nanga Parbat, it has one sharp, prominent peak — 25,560 feet above the sea, and nearly 20,000 above the Kanjut river — whose granite crags tower high*

*over the surrounding vast glaciers and snow-fields. Surely no military expedition ever before penetrated so sublime a mountain region as that which now lay before us.*

Durand had mounted an expedition to subdue the slave-trading and raiding of the rival Hunza and Nagar kingdoms, a few miles from Chalt up the Hunza River gorge after they reneged on a treaty they had signed with the British. There was no doubting the valour of the Hunzakuts. Colonel Durand found them redoubtable and indomitable fighters. Armed with no more than 100 guns, they encased garnets in lead to fashion bullets.

The 2,000 Gurkhas, Sikhs, and Pukhtuns led by Durand's officers, including Knight, were equally courageous in what Knight described as 'one of the most brilliant little campaigns in military history'. Fought in the most difficult terrain imaginable, it was a month-long epic of high adventure and courage on both sides. It ended when a British force climbed a 1,000-foot-high sheer face to overwhelm the enemy's final bastion. One outcome was the award of the Victoria Cross to two British officers for conspicuous valour during the campaign.

Ever since, Hunza and Nagar, fabled once-upon-a-time kingdoms out of a fairy-tale of feuding princes, eternal life, and treasure troves of gold and jewels, have been at peace with themselves and the rest of the world.

The valley emerges suddenly around a bend after a seemingly endless series of daunting, barren gorges — a living fantasy so medievally magic and colourful no artist could envision it.

Yet it has existed for a thousand years. The cliffside ledges on which the castles, palaces, and tiny towns of these kingdoms are perched, served as a stupendous natural fortress. Dominating all is the massive yet somehow slender, soaring profile of Rakaposhi. Its snows are a gleaming kaleidoscope of changing colours throughout the day as the sun shifts across the horizon and filters through the billowing clouds that boil and fret around its peaks.

The 30,000 citizens that live beneath were the liegemen of the Amirs of Hunza, whose successor even today still retains many of his traditional powers. He ruled until 1974, when Hunza became part of Pakistan. For the locals little has changed — yet. But with the opening of the Karakoram Highway, another avalanche, that of tourists, threatens their captivating castled kingdom, perhaps even more than the thundering rocks that powder the mountain slopes in their passing fury.

Set 8,000 feet above sea level, a tapestry of stonewall, terraced fields the size of tennis courts, sublime in their springtime beauty, surrounds the town, which itself climbs up the valley's steep slopes in a series of terraces. As the

144

Opposite: Country bus
passengers halted by a
landslide that washed away the
Karakoram Highway refresh
themselves in a roadside
stream.

season changes so do the colours, from springtime green to high summer yellow to autumn gold and orange and winter grey.

These little towns with their flat-topped houses and tiny fields and orchards with ant-like figures working their ox-teams so far beneath The Roof of the World give a sense of the majestic and infinite scale of matchless nature.

For Himalayan mountaineer Eric Shipton it was 'the ultimate manifestation of mountain grandeur' — the most spectacular country he had ever seen. Few would argue.

There's some truth to the myth. Scientists discovered that the Hunzakuts almost monotonous winter diet of dried fruit — principally apricots — and the mineral-rich waters of its river certainly promote longevity. Many centenarians still work their fields in Hunza.

The Amir, and virtually all his subjects, are followers of the Aga Khan, a conversion that took place some time in the nineteenth century.

But there was little contentment in the old days. The Mirs were crafty, fratricidal rulers who held their subjects in bondage. They were not averse to bickering one among the other — as might be expected of those with a penchant for sneaking to a brother's bedroom and cutting his throat or slipping poison into his food or drink.

Eventually, Hunza was divided in a feud between two of the brothers — one to rule Hunza with burning hatred of Nagar, the other to rule Nagar with burning hatred of Hunza. Only the river and the sheer cliffs of a few miles of the Hispar Valley where Nagar stands separated them. But when they were not marauding the trade caravans, killing the leaders and pillaging the goods, they every so often went to war against each other.

Claiming lineage with Alexander the Great, a name which has echoed down the ages in their oral history, the Amirs had an overwhelming conceit about their importance and the size of their empires which they rated as only slightly smaller than that of China.

Long ago, the capital was at Baltit, which sits at the head of the lovely side valley of Ultar beneath the tail of the glacier of the same name. Set far back from Rakaposhi, with the great peaks of the Karakoram framing the foreground of the valley, the panorama seen here is unsurpassed. One of these peaks, a slender granite obelisk that stretches 2,000 feet above its base, is known as Princess Bubuli's throne. The soughing of the wind that whines and screams around it during the fury of a storm is said to be her mournful cry of despair at being imprisoned so long.

For the princess, says local folklore, was married to a Tibetan warlord who returned home to fight a war, leaving his wife seated on the top of the peak with a cockerel and a bag of millet. As he rode away he instructed her to give

Opposite: Men of the Frontier
Works Organization clear a
massive landslide on the
Karakoram Highway near
Khunjerab Pass.

**149**

Opposite: Ancient carvings at Ganesh, Hunza Valley.

the cockerel one grain a year 'and when the grain is done I shall return'.

But since he also told the poor princess he would return 'yesterday and tomorrow, when donkeys grow horns, when millstones sprout beards, and rivers flow uphill' no wonder she remains, her lament echoing in the lonely vastness around the peak.

Above Baltit, reminiscent of much architecture found in Tibet, stands the 900-year-old whitewashed house that was the palace of the Hunza Amirs until 1960 when the prince moved into an elegant, new, white-roofed stone palace. This is set in a staircase garden of shrubs and gracious trees and the dynasty's pennant still flutters from the roof at festivals and other celebrations, at Karimabad, the new capital.

Directly beneath the old palace, leaning dangerously downhill, a mosque renowned for the glory of its carved pillars and crossbeams perches precariously on a slope.

Impressive too, is Altit's 1,000-year-old fort an equal distance from Karimabad. It stands at the edge of a sheer thousand-foot drop above the Hunza River and you reach it on a four-wheel drive trail that takes you through a series of terrifying hairpins and across a swinging suspension bridge. Enough, even if you never suffered before, to make you a victim of vertigo. The fort's watch tower dates back to AD 909.

Along the Karakoram Highway near Karimabad you can explore an ancient village, Ganesh, with its carved mosque and the old swimming pool in which all Hunza children of yore took mandatory lessons. In fact, swimming the Hunza in near spate was a major part of their initiation rites. There are also some ancient inscriptions, in four old scripts, Kharoshthi, Sogdian, Gupta, and Tibetan, carved on the rocks at Ganesh between 2,000 and 1,500 years ago by travellers on the Silk Route.

There are also more ancient rock carvings of hunting and ibex. It's hereabouts too that you'll come across the mining operations which exploit Hunza's reserves of mineral wealth — the precious and semi-precious gemstones, including ruby, mined in the hills and scooped from the dry river beds.

The most remote village in this region is Hispar, perched beneath the tail of one of the Pamir Knot's most forbidding glaciers, parallel to that of the Chogo Lungma Glacier. The Hispar leads up to a daunting 17,550-foot-high pass that trails down to the Biafo Glacier and through Askole to the Baltoro.

Only the fittest can survive this trek, even in high summer when crashing avalanches and landslides threaten any second. But it is the way to Baltistan. Most, however, will take the easier route from Gilgit, along the sister road to the Karakoram Highway that winds around the base of Nanga Parbat to

Overleaf: Summer blooms above the jade waters of Lake Buret, near Gulmit.

Opposite: Apricots laid out to dry in sun on the flat roofs of Altit Village, Hunza Valley.

Opposite: Bojoahaghur Dunasir's great summit dominates the skyline above Altit fort.

Overleaf: Dirt road carved out of a sheer cliff face in the Hindu Kush.

Skardu and Little Tibet, heartland of the greatest assembly of mountains that stand on this earth.

Since time began, Baltistan has remained isolated from the rest of the world. It was first mentioned in the annals of an AD 747 Chinese military expedition to aid Ladakh against a threatened invasion from Tibet. Fascinated, the ancient Chinese geographers named it the 'Tibet of the Apricots' — because of the abundance of this fruit that grew there, and still does. Long a Buddhist country, Islam was embraced in the fifteenth century and during the Mughal era it was annexed to India. But when Aurangzeb died it soon reverted to its isolated, independent ways, only to come under a succession of local rulers — Dogras, Sikhs, and Afghans — finally coming into the kingdom of Kashmir.

From the upper edge of a glacier, Vigne became probably the first European to stumble on this limbo land.

*. . . through a long sloping vista formed of barren peaks, of savage shapes and various colours, in which the milky whiteness of the gypsum was contrasted the red tint of those that contained iron — I the first European that had ever beheld them (so I believe), gazed downwards . . . upon the sandy plains and green orchards . . . with a sense of mingled pride and pleasure.*

At Independence in 1947, however, Baltistan chose to join Pakistan, although India consistently contends the icy slopes of the Siachen Glacier and the heights around 24,480-foot-high Teram Kangris.

There is no higher land in all the world than this once-forgotten, unknown kingdom. Its highest point reaches 28,250 feet and there is nothing below 7,000 feet — and at that altitude land is rare and surprising. It seems nothing could live, let alone fight, within this frozen embrace where sub-zero winds blow constantly, often demoniacally, night and day, carrying snow and ice in their breath.

Yet, astonishingly, the valley beneath the plane as you approach Skardu is a pure replica of the Sahara — an area of shifting sand dunes. Indeed, from the air, all the land around Skardu takes on the appearance of a sea-shore — visible evidence that until fairly recently the valley around Skardu itself, so fair and broad the jagged peaks surrounding it seem almost benevolent, was a lake.

Not until October 1978, with the completion of the 170-kilometre-long Shahrah-e-Skardu, did Baltistan have any permanent access to the rest of the world, and even in the 1980s the citizens retained their self-sufficiency and independence, aloof from the twentieth century and its wonders. So formidable in the scale of its colour and texture, savagery and desolation is the Indus gorge out of Skardu that not even hardy Baltis ventured to cross it.

The Shahrah-e-Skardu is one of the most dramatic roads in the world, following the narrow, dark, bleak, and stupendously high ravine of the Indus for mile after mile. Never a blade of grass relieves the monotony of the hostile rock. Only the jade-green river, tumbling and foaming in stretches of white water, relieves the grey-brown, sere, and unrelenting walls of boulder-strewn rock, scree, and cliffs.

For centuries, traders and expeditions ventured through the gorge along a footpath so narrow that in some parts it simply ended in space. These were bridged with fragile timber to form a precarious foothold in the sky. A simple slip and man or beast plunged 2,000 feet or more to their death.

In winter waterfalls hang frozen in gigantic 3,000-foot-long icicles of massive thickness waiting for the spring thaw to release them from their bondage of suspended animation.

In some sections the advance parties worked on tracks where curves were so severe that jeeps had to make five- or seven-point turns, many failing and falling into the boiling waters below. Landslides and rockfalls are an almost daily occurrence. Winds tore tents to shreds and the workers faced summer highs of more than 108°F and winter lows of minus 30°F.

A Swedish engineer called in for advice took one look at the gorge — 'what kind of mountains are these? . . . no vegetation . . . no trees . . . only miles and miles of black rock' — and said, 'The only advice I can give is not to make a road here.'

Like its larger sister, the Karakoram Highway, it represents one of the world's major feats of civil engineering construction and already Skardu, long a Mecca for the high altitude mountaineer, has become a major tourist resort as the coaches, cars, and jeeps flood down the road across more than twenty bridges to the town.

But in the 1980s, however, many visitors opted for the sixty-minute flight from Rawalpindi which flies along the Indus past Nanga Parbat, then banks sharply starboard to follow the Indus through one of the narrowest ravines ever flown by a civil airline — the walls rise thousands of feet above, dwarfing the puny passenger plane.

Leaving the plane, the most immediate impression is that of disorientation. The valley and the rock and the desert plains have no likeness to any other landscape — as if the Sahara had been dropped down between massive walls of rock. There are no perspectives. So complete is the circle of mountains everything narrows and the eye is ever confused.

Lying within this ring of 17,000-foot-high mountains that glimmer through the haze in varying shades of purple, grey, and ochre, the jade river Indus snakes sinuously between the ribboned, wind-blown sand dunes close

159

beneath a 200-foot-high island of massive rock. It's here that Skardu straggles along the plateau.

Its real attraction is as gateway to the grandest sight in all nature — Concordia, the amphitheatre of ten of the world's thirty greatest mountains, the adjacent glaciers and peaks — and its closeness to Lake Satpara, one of the hidden pearls of Little Tibet.

Its emerald waters gleaming in the sun, it lies at the foot of a majestic mountain. An island in its centre makes a lovely summer picnic spot. But, thirty-two kilometres downstream, it's Kachura Lake, renamed *Shangri-la* by the owner of the hotel that sits on its meadowlands of wild flowers and blossoming orchards, which perhaps has claim to be the most lovely spot in Baltistan — the more so because of its verdant contrast to the bleak sterility all around.

In the crisp alpine air there surely can be few other places for the angler which lay claim to such an impressive setting. The lake teems with fat, sporting trout, as do many of the lakes and rivers.

Above the capital stands an ancient sixteenth-century fortress, a network of dark corridors and inky recesses linked by wooden staircases. Below, the unimpressive town stretches for several kilometres of tree-lined streets and roads, but only the bazaar will invite the visitor to linger.

Capital of a kingdom that held its people in bondage for a century and a half, scattered areas of the valley blossom in the summer with cherries, apricots, almonds, and pears, and the fields yield rice, maize, wheat, and fodder for the animals. Villages of stone and timber houses with dark and narrow stairwells, riven by gloomy, unlit alleys, cluster within the embrace of the fertile terraces — glittering jewels set in the tarnished silver clasp of the barren granite cliffs and soaring peaks.

Such interludes of fertility are brief and far between. Basically, Baltistan is an alpine desert, perhaps the most forbidding and fearful landscape anywhere on earth. To be lost on foot in this wilderness, you think as your plane drones on, must surely be to abandon all hope. But the sheer scale and vastness of its perpendicular perspectives lures more and more visitors each year.

Keay writes of the 'overall impression of rock and sand, harsh white light and biting dry wind':

*Natural vegetation is a rare and transitory phenomenon; cultivation is just an artificial patchwork of fields suspended from a contour-clinging irrigation duct or huddled on the triangular surface of a fan of alluvial soil washed down from the mountains.*

163

South-east of Skardu, the Khaplu Valley winds away to Ladakh for 100 kilometres along perhaps the most treacherous road in Baltistan. But what views reward the effort. The ever-changing landscapes follow the sandy valley floor, black mountains reflecting in the waters of the Shyok River. On the slopes, little communities have carved their terraced fields and homes out of the mountainside, diverting the waters along a network of ancient irrigation aqueducts.

The capital of this valley, distinctively Tibetan in its people and architecture, is spread out along the greenest and broadest bowl of the valley, an arena that for the non-trekker it is the keypoint of the entire visit to Baltistan. For only in Khaplu, so high and close together are the region's other valleys, do you catch sight of the *raison d'être* for any visit to Baltistan — its mountains. Here, in the early morning, as the sun slopes above the eastern horizon, its rays burst in a dazzling shower of diamonds on the scintillating peak of mighty 25,660-foot-high Masherbrum.

North of Skardu lies the vale of Shigar: a landscape of gentle, smiling fields dominated by a dreamy wooden village and an ancient carved mosque. Now the track climbs ever higher and the valley walls close in until you reach Dassu, a narrow bowl of a valley no wider, it seems, than two or three miles, completely encircled by a range of snow-capped peaks reaching heights of more than 20,000 feet, looking every minute as if they may fall over and crash down on this lost horizon. The land is sparse and the villagers hardy. Many work as porters and supply trains of the major mountaineering expeditions, for Dassu is the starting point for the assault on the mountains of Concordia.

Trekking in Baltistan demands more in terms of fitness and physical endurance than anywhere else. Only the fittest can explore its valleys, glaciers, highlands, and lofty peaks. No human can live permanently above 15,000 feet. The body's metabolism is unable to replenish red blood cells. Nor does it renew itself. After days, even the fittest are close to total exhaustion, their faces tanned dark by the ultraviolet rays and the stinging wind, their systems totally debilitated.

Many succumb to potentially lethal altitude sicknesses like pulmonary and cerebral oedema — fluid on the lungs and brain. As the rarefied air cuts down the oxygen which produces vital red blood cells, symptoms vary from breathlessness, nausea, disorientation, and slurred speech. Without swift descent and attention the result is often fatal.

Yet, even at the highest points, soldiers of the Pakistan Army keep steadfast vigilance over their nation: defying long winter's night, isolated in tiny crevasses and frozen nooks perched thousands of feet above sheer dizzying drops, battered by uncessant gale force winds on the highest front line in the

Previous pages: Shifting sand dunes 7,000 feet above sea level form a pure desert beneath Skardu's encircling snowcapped sentinel peaks — an almost perfect replica of Africa's Sahara.

Opposite: Plane and poplar trees stand tall in the arid slopes of the Baltoro Valley and shade a rare oasis of terraced fields near Dassu.

Overleaf: Where mountains preen themselves, their debris litters the brief summer flush of grain in the terraced fields of Askole, Pakistan's highest and most remote village — the last human settlement before the march up Baltoro Glacier to Concordia and the Roof of The World.

history of human conflict.

Their support systems — tenuous lifelines maintained by helicopter and pack beasts — characterize the unswerving skills and courage displayed by the Pakistan Armed Forces. Daily, Puma choppers of the Pakistan Army fly along the narrow valleys that intersect these mountain ranges, tossed and buffeted by the winds that channel down these stupendous ravines, carrying food, ammunition, and fuel. Below these frail aircraft, trains of donkey stumble along precipitous mountain trails and over treacherous glaciers to stock up forward depots and base camps.

It was in May 1948 that this young army was sent to reinforce the Kashmiri resistance fighters in their struggle to repel the Indian troops who had been despatched to annex Kashmir to the new Indian Union. Quickly, these soldiers seized Poonch, Muzzafarabad, Mirpur, Gilgit, and Skardu.

Ever since, India has been facing off Pakistan on ground that morally, by the wishes of its people, should be part of Pakistan, and the issue has continued to bedevil Indo-Pak relationships.

On the 120-minute flight to Gore you get an understanding of the dangers they treat as routine. Mountains, 20,000 feet high, rise sheer in front and on either side of the Puma as it manoeuvres through the valleys. Waterfalls that plunge 2,000 to 3,000 feet hang frozen in suspended animation, waiting for the summer melt. The Puma banks sharply, turning to starboard, to enter the valley carved out of the millenniums by the Baltoro Glacier and land at Gore. From its spectacular birthplace in Concordia at the base of the K-2 and the Masherbrum range, it flows for more than fifty-eight kilometres.

For the tourist, the trek along the Baltoro Glacier culminates in a camp in the 15,180-foot-high Concordia — a meeting place of gigantic glaciers that may well deserve the dubious soubriquet 'Crossroads of the World'.

Baltoro, its surface riven with crevasses and pitted with corrugations that from afar look like the rutted tracks made by some monstrous vehicle, has many tributary glaciers. At Concordia three component glaciers meet, forming the proscenium for the most spectacular natural theatre in the world.

Within a radius of twenty-five kilometres, stand ten of the world's thirty highest peaks. 'They line its sides and close its easternmost end like high priests guarding the Holy of Holies,' writes Keay.

That so much is known of this impenetrable fortress is due to the courage, persistence and skills of surveyors like Godwin-Austen and William Henry Johnson in a drawn-out marathon that became an essay in scientific genius. The Kashmir operations of the Grand Trigonometrical Series of the Survey of India began in 1855 — the zenith of one of the nineteenth century's greatest scientific projects. It was, as John Keay wrote, an incredible achievement.

174

Opposite: Above the Baltoro Glacier tendrils of cloud kiss the summit of 22,176-feet-high Biarchedi above the Masherbrum Pass, centre.

Opposite: Mighty peaks rise up above the Baltoro Glacier, foreground. From left to right they are — Trango Towers, Baltoro Cathedrals, Lopsang group, Mustagh Tower, far distant at 23,863 feet, and Broad Peak, 26,405 feet.

Overleaf top: Helicopter moves slowly above the surface of Concordia.

Overleaf bottom: From a cave overlooking Siachen Glacier.

Overleaf right: Pakistan Air Force F16 leads two Mirages over the great massif of 26,660-feet-high Nanga Parbat, westernmost anchor of the mighty Himalaya.

*The surveyor had to cover all the ground. He was after vantage points.*
*Across empty, trackless regions he moved from one high peak to another. . . .*
*as much a mountaineer as a traveller.*

They had to hump heavy equipment, including 100-pound theodolites, with them — over mountains and across raging rivers — from one high point to another. Setting up a 'trig' station in the most forbidding place, the surveyor then computed the angles between one base line and his station and a third point. One of these would then form the next base line. So accurate were these measurements that a series carried over hundreds of kilometres erred by no more than a fraction of a centimetre for each base kilometre.

Sometimes, at altitudes of 15,000 feet or more, they had to dig down through eleven or twelve feet of snow to find a stable, level base on which to build a stone pillar for the theodolite.

If they were lucky, wrote Keay, they might complete their work in a day or so:

*The clouds would break. A vast array of snow-clad peaks would rise from the blanket of mist in the valleys . . . Then from a distant peak, indistinguishable from a hundred others, would shine the tell-tale pinpoint of light, the 'sight never to be forgotten of a well-served heliotrope'.*

Through blizzard, frost, and storm the surveyors moved forward, victim of altitude sickness, frostbite, and snow-blindness. At times, lightning set their hair ablaze.

From one of these vantage points in September 1856, Captain T. G. Montgomerie caught his first sight of K-2 and Masherbrum some 225 kilometres away and took bearings on them, mistakenly calculating that Masherbrum was the higher of the two. Twice more in the next three years, however, other surveyors took bearings from different locations on the two peaks and from these K–2's height was calculated as 28,727 feet. Montgomerie concluded:

*'The peak may therefore be considered the second highest in the world.'*

It was Godwin-Austen who first surveyed Baltoro. 'Up this broad aisle of ice,' wrote Keay, 'Godwin-Austen and his men now made their painful progress.' His view blocked by the tangle of peaks that guard this noble giant, he climbed high on Masherbrum and at the point beyond which he could not advance saw the mountain in all its glory. 'There with not a particle of cloud to hide it stood the great peak K-2.'

Opposite: 19,729-feet-high Mitre Peak, a spire of treacherous, crumbling rock, stands sentinel at the junction of Concordia with the Baltoro Glacier.

Godwin-Austen's success rested not on his scientific skills alone. He was also a magnificent mountaineer — he had to be. Year after year, wrote Keay, he broke the world's altitude record — from 19,600 feet to 19,900 feet; from 20,600 feet to 21,000 feet, at which height he built a 'trig' station; finally to stand at 22,300 feet. Four of his stations were the world's highest for more than sixty years.

K-2, only 773 feet lower than Everest, is considered the most challenging and beautiful of all mountains. First conquered by an Italian expedition on 31 July 1954, its perils are many — avalanche, landslide, frequent and unpredictable storm, and savage winds. It has claimed more than fifteen lives.

Its neighbours are equally beautiful and almost as challenging. Broad Peak, 26,400 feet, was first climbed in 1955; Gasherbrum, 26,470 feet in 1958; and Masherbrum, 25,660 feet, in 1960.

Reinhold Messner, the only man to have climbed all fourteen peaks that stand above 26,250 feet rates K-2 the toughest of all. In his ascent in company with others he recorded his thoughts:

*Ahead of us, there it stands, this summit pyramid. It all makes absolute sense without being at all rational or irrational. . . . The feeling sometimes comes to me that I have already died and therefore have nothing left to lose. It washes over me in the early mornings when I awake from a restless, dreamless sleep. I busy myself and feel inwardly calm and content. Nothing worse can happen to me.*

But why he climbs against such odds is well explained. In reach of the second-highest point on earth he was overwhelmed by his emotions. 'I am no longer myself, and yet once again I am.'

*The wonderful twilight enfolds me and fills me with freedom — also perhaps with longing and with sadness. It is as if a time awaited me, which has yet to come — the twilight over the valleys.*

He has seen the long, long shadow of K-2 lengthening in the evenings until it casts its pyramid profile many, many kilometres to the east, a unique phenomenon, a spectacle no words can describe and that only a brave few will ever experience, on The Roof of the World, where men and mountains meet and continents collide.

Opposite: Winds blowing at more than 160 kilometres an hour send a plume of spindrift flying from a pyramid peak in the Karakoram.

Following pages: K2 base camp in the Concordia amphitheatre. The saddle, centre background, is the Sella Pass; Pages 184-185: Ice walls sparkle on the daunting, jagged ridge and summit of Nanga Parbat, considered the most dangerous of the world's fourteen-highest mountains; Pages 186-187: Lama helicopter jockeys along Concordia beneath Mitre Peak with the ridgeback summit of 25,027-feet-high Chogolisa, extreme left, above Vigne Glacier. Naating Glacier is extreme right; Pages 188-189: Side glacier streams down into the mainstream Godwin-Austen Glacier; Pages 190-191: Concordia in the foreground, Godwin-Austen Glacier stretches to the base of cloud-girdled K2 with, at left, Angelus Peak, 22,491 feet, and, right, the world's twelfth-highest point Broad Peak, 26,405 feet; Page 192: Sunburst over the Godwin-Austen glacier near K2.